# Table of Contents

Chapter1. Introduction to Smart Grocery Shopping

Chapter 2. Your Shopping List

Chapter 3. Shopping Your Pantry First

Chapter 4. Things To Remember

Chapter 5. Buying Generic Brands for Savings

Chapter 6. The Best Time for Shopping

Chapter 7. Do Grocery Shopping Without Kids

Chapter 8. Selecting Between Online and In-Store Purchases

Chapter 9. Shopping Off-Brand Items

Chapter 10. Maximizing Savings with Digital Tools

Chapter 11. Maximizing Savings with Bulk Purchases

Chapter 12. Avoiding Impulse Buys

Chapter 13. Freezing Fresh Produce for Long-Term Savings

Chapter 14. Ask Others for Information

Chapter 15. Benefits of Buying Frozen Produce

Chapter 16. Make Arrangements for Quick Meals

Chapter 17. The Importance of Keeping Receipts

Chapter 18. Seasonal Grocery Planning for Absences

Chapter 19. Smart Beverage Choices to Save Money

Chapter 20. Combining Foods for Savings

Chapter 21. Economical Homemade Delights

Chapter 22. Check Expiry Dates

Chapter 23. Tips for Selecting Fresh Produce

Chapter 24. Tips for Selecting Good Quality Meat

Chapter 25. Sample Products Before Buying

Chapter 26. Grocery Shopping with Dietary Restrictions

Chapter 27. Positive Grocery Shopping Etiquette

Chapter 28. Gradual Shopping for Special Occasions

Chapter 29. Communication with Store Staff

Chapter 30. Shopping with Organization

Chapter 31. Using Thermal Bags and Cooler Boxes

Chapter 32. Late-Night Grocery Discounts

Chapter 33. Avoid Excess Buying of Discounted Items
Chapter 34. Efficient Meal Planning
Chapter 35. DIY Kitchen Staples for Savings and Flavor
Chapter 36. Healthy Eating on a Budget
Chapter 37. Buying at Farmers Markets
Chapter 38. Smart Grocery Shopping Abroad
Chapter 39. Specialty and Ethnic Grocery Shopping
Chapter 40. Making Organic and Sustainable Choices
Chapter 41. Cooking for One or Two
Chapter 42.  Emergency Preparedness
Chapter 43. Snack and Lunchbox Ideas
Chapter 44. Smart Unit Price Shopping Guide
Chapter 45. Maximizing Savings with Seasonal Shopping
Chapter 46. Spend Within Your Budget
Chapter 47. The Art of Making Food Combinations
Chapter 48. Some Important Considerations
Chapter 49: Understanding Store Layouts and Strategies
Chapter 50: Eco-Friendly Grocery Shopping Practices
Chapter 51: Grocery Shopping for Special Diets
Chapter 52: Last But Not Least

# Chapter 1: Introduction

In today's world, grocery shopping isn't just about picking up food—it's a skill that can significantly impact your health, budget, and overall well-being. Clever grocery shopping goes beyond simply filling your cart; it involves strategic planning, mindful decision-making, and an understanding of how to maximize value while minimizing costs. This chapter introduces the concept of clever grocery shopping, exploring why it's essential, the benefits it offers, and how it can transform your approach to food and finances.

In recent years, people have learned a lot about managing their lives in light of rising living costs. We work hard to earn money, but it's a pity if we can't use our money in the right way. Therefore, it's very important to use every bit of our money in a clever way. Grocery shopping is one of the main monthly expenditures, and there can surely be a considerable amount saved on groceries that we can use in other ways or just add to our savings. Clever shoppers are well aware of the realities of life; therefore, they never miss an opportunity to save money wherever they can.

Clever grocery shopping is more than a task; it's a lifestyle choice that integrates health, finance, and sustainability. By adopting strategic practices like meal planning, budgeting, and mindful shopping, you can optimize your grocery shopping experience to save time, money, and resources. It's important to learn about the concept of clever grocery shopping and its importance, benefits, and practical implications for everyday life. This book is specially written to give you specific strategies, tips, and insights that will empower you to become a savvy grocery shopper and reap the many rewards it offers. Because it all has a huge impact on the way we shop, eat, and live.

## What is Smart Grocery Shopping?

Smart grocery shopping is a methodical approach to buying food and household essentials that focuses on efficiency, budgeting, and nutrition. It's about making informed choices based on your needs and priorities while considering factors like quality, price, and sustainability. This approach involves several key practices:

**Meal Planning:** Planning meals in advance helps you create a shopping list that aligns with your dietary goals and budget. By mapping out what you'll eat for the week or even the month, you can ensure you buy only what you need and reduce food waste.

**Budgeting:** Setting a grocery budget and sticking to it is fundamental to smart shopping. It involves balancing your income with your expenses, allocating a portion for groceries, and finding ways to make your money go further.

**Strategic Shopping:** Knowing when and where to shop for the best deals, utilizing discounts, coupons, and loyalty programs, and choosing cost-effective options like store brands or bulk purchases are all part of strategic shopping.

**Nutritional Awareness:** Prioritizing nutrient-dense foods, fresh produce, and healthy ingredients ensures that you're not only saving money but also supporting your overall health and well-being.

## Why Do We Need Clever Grocery Shopping?

The need for clever grocery shopping arises from the intersection of health, finance, and practicality in daily life:

**Health Benefits:** By focusing on nutritious foods and minimizing processed items, clever grocery shopping promotes better health outcomes. A balanced diet rich in fruits, vegetables, lean proteins, and whole grains supports physical well-being, boosts energy levels, and enhances cognitive function.

**Financial Savings:** Clever grocery shopping is a cornerstone of financial management. It helps you stretch your grocery budget, avoid unnecessary spending, and make informed choices that save money over time. These savings can be redirected towards other essential expenses or savings goals.

**Time Efficiency:** Planning meals and shopping strategically saves time in the long run. By reducing the frequency of shopping trips, minimizing impulse buys, and organizing your shopping list efficiently, you can streamline the grocery shopping process and free up time for other activities.

## Benefits of Smart Grocery Shopping

The benefits of adopting smart and efficient approach to grocery shopping extend far beyond the immediate task of buying food:

**Financial Freedom:** By mastering clever grocery shopping techniques, you gain control over one of your most significant household expenses. This financial discipline extends to other areas of life, empowering you to make informed financial decisions and prioritize savings.

**Health and Wellness:** Choosing fresh, nutrient-dense foods supports your physical health and well-being. Clever grocery shopping encourages mindful eating habits and reduces reliance on processed foods, which are often high in unhealthy fats, sugars, and additives.

**Skill Development:** Learning to plan meals, budget effectively, and navigate grocery stores efficiently are valuable life skills. These skills translate into better organization, improved decision-making, and enhanced problem-solving abilities in various aspects of your personal and professional life.

**Environmental Impact:** Making sustainable choices—such as buying local produce, reducing food waste, and using reusable shopping bags—contributes to environmental conservation. Clever grocery shopping encourages responsible consumption practices that minimize ecological footprints.

**Educational Value:** Engaging in clever grocery shopping expands your knowledge about food, nutrition, and culinary skills. It encourages the exploration of new ingredients, recipes, and cooking techniques, fostering a deeper appreciation for food preparation and its impact on health.

## How Smart Grocery Shopping Saves Time and Money

Efficiency is at the core of clever grocery shopping practices, leading to both time and monetary savings:

**Reduced Food Waste:** By planning meals and buying only what you need, you minimize the chances of food spoilage and waste. This not only cuts costs but also lessens the environmental footprint.

**Streamlined Shopping Experience:** Organizing your shopping list by aisle, utilizing technology such as grocery apps, and knowing store layouts can cut down on time spent wandering aisles and searching for items.

**Financial Planning:** Setting a grocery budget and tracking expenses helps you allocate funds effectively, ensuring that you stay within your financial limits while meeting nutritional needs.

**Economic Benefits:** By supporting local producers, choosing seasonal ingredients, and shopping during sales or promotions, you capitalize on cost-effective opportunities and maximize purchasing power.

## The Interconnected Benefits of Smart Grocery Shopping

Beyond the immediate advantages of saving money and time, smart grocery shopping cultivates broader benefits that enrich daily life:

**Healthier Eating Habits:** By prioritizing nutritious foods and minimizing processed items, you create a foundation for long-term health and vitality. A diet rich in vitamins, minerals, and antioxidants supports immune function, reduces the risk of chronic diseases, and promotes overall well-being.

**Financial Savvy:** Mastering the art of clever grocery shopping enhances financial literacy and responsibility. It teaches budgeting skills, encourages mindful spending habits, and instills a sense of financial empowerment.

**Environmental Consciousness:** Making sustainable food choices—such as opting for organic produce, reducing plastic packaging, and supporting eco-friendly brands—contributes to environmental sustainability. Clever grocery shopping aligns consumption practices with environmental stewardship, reducing carbon footprints, and preserving natural resources.

**Educational Growth:** Engaging in meal planning, exploring diverse cuisines, and experimenting with new ingredients fosters culinary creativity and expands culinary knowledge. It encourages lifelong learning and exploration of food cultures, promoting a deeper appreciation for the culinary arts and food diversity.

# Chapter 2: Your Shopping List

Going grocery shopping without a list is like starting your journey without a map or itinerary. It's a fundamental principle of clever shopping that ensures you not only get what you need but also optimize your time, energy, and finances. A well-prepared list serves as your guide, helping you navigate the aisles with purpose and efficiency.

The importance of a grocery list cannot be overstated. It begins long before you step into the store. Ideally, it starts with meal planning—a process where you map out your meals for the week or even the month ahead. Meal planning allows you to identify precisely what ingredients you'll need, ensuring that nothing essential is overlooked. By visualizing your meals in advance, you can create a comprehensive list that covers all your dietary requirements and preferences.

Beyond meal planning, your list should include more than just groceries. It can include household essentials like cleaning supplies, toiletries, and pet food. This wise approach ensures that your shopping trip is comprehensive and that you won't need to make additional stops later, saving both time and fuel.

An effective grocery list should be dynamic and responsive. It should evolve as your needs change throughout the week. As you run out of staples or notice items nearing depletion, add them immediately to your list. This proactive approach prevents last-minute scrambles and eliminates the risk of forgetting crucial items.

Moreover, keeping a running list between shopping trips allows you to take advantage of sales and promotions. By adding items to your list as you notice them, you can capitalize on discounts when they arise. This strategy not only saves money but also encourages smart budgeting and planning.

The act of writing a list is not just a practical exercise but also a mental one. It forces you to think critically about what you truly need versus what you might want impulsively. This mindfulness reduces the likelihood of making unnecessary purchases and helps you stick to your budgetary constraints.

Organizing your list strategically can further enhance your shopping efficiency. Group items by categories such as produce, dairy, meats, pantry staples, and frozen foods to mirror the layout of your preferred grocery store. This systematic approach minimizes backtracking and ensures that you move through the store in a logical, streamlined manner.

Another benefit of maintaining a list is its role in reducing food waste. By purchasing only what you need for planned meals and essentials, you minimize the chances of perishable items going unused and eventually being discarded. This not only conserves resources but also supports sustainable consumption practices.

Furthermore, a well-kept grocery list serves as a historical record of your household's consumption patterns. Over time, it allows you to identify trends in your buying habits, such as seasonal variations or changes in dietary preferences. Armed with this knowledge, you can refine your meal planning and shopping strategies to better align with your family's evolving needs.

In essence, your grocery list is not only valuable; it's a tool for empowerment and efficiency. It empowers you to take control of your shopping experience, maximize savings, and maintain order in your household.

Indeed, good shopping list-making not only simplifies your trips to the grocery store but also cultivates smart habits that extend into other areas of your life. Smart grocery shopping begins with a list—a simple yet powerful tool that transforms the way you shop, eat, and manage your resources.

# Chapter 3: Shopping Your Pantry First

Shopping your pantry first is a strategic approach to grocery shopping that begins with assessing what ingredients and items you already have at home before making a trip to the store. It involves taking inventory of your pantry or kitchen storage to identify what is available, ranging from canned goods and dry staples like pasta and rice to spices, oils, and sauces. This practice is not only about organization but also about minimizing waste and maximizing the use of resources you already possess.

The primary aim of shopping your pantry first is twofold: to reduce food waste and to save money. By checking your pantry before heading to the store, you can avoid purchasing duplicate items or ingredients you already have. This helps you use up older items before they expire and ensures that you make the most of your grocery budget by only purchasing what is necessary. It's a proactive approach that encourages thoughtful meal planning and prevents the accumulation of excess food that might go unused.

To effectively shop your pantry, start by conducting a thorough inventory of what you currently have stocked. Note down items that are running low or nearing their expiration date. This inventory serves as the foundation for planning meals based on what ingredients are already available. You can explore recipes that incorporate these pantry staples, allowing you to create meals without needing to buy additional items.

Creativity in cooking often flourishes when you shop your pantry first. Discovering new meal ideas by combining existing ingredients can lead to innovative dishes that are both satisfying and resourceful. This practice encourages culinary experimentation and can help diversify your menu without added expense.

For perishable items like fresh produce or dairy products, prioritize using these ingredients first to minimize spoilage. Incorporating them into your meal planning ensures that you're not only reducing waste but also optimizing the nutritional value of your meals. This approach supports sustainable consumption habits by emphasizing the use of what you have before acquiring more.

After reviewing your pantry inventory and planning your meals accordingly, refine your shopping list. Update it with only the items you need to buy, taking into account what you've already stocked at home. This focused approach helps streamline your grocery trip, saving time and avoiding impulse purchases that can inflate your bill.

Shopping your pantry first is not just about what you buy; it's a mindset that promotes efficiency, budget-consciousness, and sustainable living. By harnessing the resources already available to you, you contribute to reducing food waste and making informed choices about your household consumption. This practice aligns with the principles of smart grocery shopping, ensuring that every trip to the store is purposeful and economical. It's an essential step towards maintaining a well-organized kitchen and maximizing the value of your grocery purchases.

# Chapter 4: Things To Remember

Shopping for groceries is not merely a routine chore; it demands energy, preparation, and a mindful approach for a successful and satisfying experience. To optimize your shopping trip and make the most of your time and effort, consider these key factors before heading to the store.

Firstly, it's important to recognize the physical demands of grocery shopping. Maneuvering through aisles, lifting items, and covering significant distances within the store can be taxing. To tackle these demands effectively, ensure you are well-rested and nourished before you begin. Having a balanced meal beforehand provides your body with the necessary energy to sustain you throughout the trip. This preparation reduces the likelihood of making impulsive purchases driven by hunger or fatigue, allowing you to shop with clarity and intention.

Equally critical is your mental state during the shopping process. Approach your grocery trip with a calm and stress-free mindset. Shopping while feeling agitated, sad, or angry can cloud your judgment and lead to hurried decisions or unnecessary purchases. Emotions significantly influence shopping behavior, potentially prompting impulsive buying or overlooking factors like quality, price, and nutritional value. Taking a moment to center yourself before entering the store enhances your shopping experience, enabling more thoughtful decision-making.

Avoiding rush-hour or hurried shopping is another key aspect of maximizing your grocery trip. When time is tight, there's a tendency to rush through aisles, hastily grabbing items without thoroughly considering their freshness or suitability. This can result in purchasing expired products or items that do not meet your needs. Moreover, hurried shopping increases the risk of forgetting items on your list or overlooking essential ingredients for planned meals. To mitigate these challenges, allocate ample time for your shopping excursion. This allows you the freedom to browse, compare options, and select items mindfully, ensuring you acquire what you truly need.

Additionally, your shopping list is instrumental in enhancing efficiency and reducing oversights. Before leaving the store, take a look at your shopping list and check if you bought everything or something else you need to buy from another grocery store before heading home. This approach not only saves time but also minimizes the chances of forgetting essential items, ensuring your trip is productive and focused.

Lastly, be mindful of your budget throughout the shopping process. Set a realistic spending limit based on your financial resources, and stick to it. This practice helps prioritize purchases, avoid unnecessary expenses, and maintain financial discipline. Utilizing coupons, taking advantage of sales, and opting for store brands can further stretch your budget without compromising quality.

Successful grocery shopping requires careful preparation, both physically and mentally. By approaching the task with awareness, adequate time, and a focused mindset, you can optimize your shopping experience, make informed choices, and ultimately enjoy the benefits of a well-stocked pantry and fridge.

# Chapter 5: Buying Generic Brands for Savings

In today's consumer landscape, generic brands have become increasingly popular as a cost-effective alternative to name-brand products. These products are characterized by their straightforward packaging and labeling, which often eschew the elaborate branding strategies employed by national brands. Instead of being marketed under flashy logos and slogans, generics focus on delivering quality products at competitive prices.

The rise of generic brands is closely tied to consumer demand for value-oriented shopping options. Grocery retailers and chains have responded by expanding their private label offerings, providing consumers with a wider array of choices that cater to various preferences and needs. These store brands, also known as private labels, are manufactured under contract by reputable suppliers and are designed to offer comparable quality to their branded counterparts.

Economically, choosing generic brands can translate into significant savings for consumers. Unlike national brands that allocate substantial resources to marketing and advertising, generic brands operate on a more streamlined business model. By minimizing these overhead costs, manufacturers can pass on the savings to consumers, making generics an attractive option for budget-conscious shoppers.

Moreover, some generic products are manufactured in the same facilities as national brands, adhering to identical quality standards. This practice ensures that consumers can enjoy products with consistent quality and performance, whether they opt for a store-brand version or a name-brand product.

When considering whether to purchase generic brands, cost comparison plays a crucial role. Generic products typically offer a lower cost per unit or per ounce compared to their branded counterparts. This financial advantage makes generics an appealing choice, especially for families and individuals looking to stretch their grocery budget without compromising on quality.

Consumer confidence in generic brands is bolstered by satisfaction guarantees offered by many retailers. These policies allow shoppers to try store-brand products risk-free and return them for a refund or exchange if they are not satisfied. Such assurances encourage consumers to explore and experiment with different generics, fostering brand loyalty based on positive shopping experiences.

Beyond financial savings, choosing generic brands offers additional benefits. Many generics are recognized for their quality parity with national brands, adhering to stringent manufacturing and safety standards. This ensures that consumers can trust the nutritional value, ingredients, and overall performance of generic products, making them a reliable choice for everyday essentials.

In practical terms, generic brands are available across a wide range of categories, from pantry staples and household goods to personal care items and medications. This accessibility and diversity allow consumers to consistently find cost-effective alternatives without compromising on their shopping preferences or needs.

Consumer trends and market studies consistently highlight the growing popularity of generic brands. The Private Label Manufacturers Association reports a steady increase in consumer preference for store brands, driven by their affordability and perceived value. Products like cereals, snacks, dairy items, and over-the-counter medications are among the top purchases in generic form, reflecting widespread consumer acceptance and satisfaction with these products.

Buying generic brands presents a practical and economical approach to grocery shopping. By leveraging cost savings, quality assurance, and consumer-friendly policies, generics offer a compelling alternative to national brands. Whether you're stocking up on household essentials or exploring new products, choosing generics can contribute to a more budget-conscious and satisfying shopping experience.

# Chapter 6: The Best Time for Shopping

Choosing the optimal time for grocery shopping can significantly impact your overall shopping experience and the quality of the products you purchase. Timing your trip strategically ensures access to fresh and well-stocked items while minimizing stress and inconvenience.

One of the primary reasons for selecting the right time for grocery shopping is the availability of fresh produce and perishable items. Early morning often proves to be the ideal time for shopping, especially for fruits, vegetables, and bakery items that are stocked fresh daily. Shopping during these hours ensures you have a wide selection of crisp, ripe produce and freshly baked goods, contributing to healthier meal choices and enhanced culinary experiences.

Moreover, morning shopping offers the advantage of fewer shoppers in the store. The early hours typically see fewer crowds, allowing you to navigate aisles more efficiently and avoid long queues at checkout counters. This reduces waiting times and streamlines the entire shopping process, enabling you to complete your purchases swiftly and with minimal hassle.

The serene atmosphere of early morning shopping also contributes to a more relaxed and enjoyable experience. With fewer people around, there is less noise and commotion, creating a tranquil environment conducive to focused decision-making. This tranquil setting allows you to browse products thoughtfully, compare options, and select items based on your preferences without feeling rushed or pressured.

Another advantage of shopping in the morning is the fresh mindset and energy you bring to the task. Starting your day with a grocery run when you are well-rested and mentally alert enhances your ability to make informed choices. A clear mind enables you to stick to your shopping list, prioritize essential items, and resist impulsive purchases, ultimately leading to more economical and efficient shopping habits.

Furthermore, the logistical aspects of morning shopping contribute to a more orderly shopping experience. Stores are typically well organized and neatly stocked in the early hours, making it easier to locate items and find everything on your list without unnecessary detours or searches. The orderly arrangement of products enhances convenience and saves time, allowing you to focus on selecting the best options available.

Additionally, early-morning shopping can offer unexpected savings opportunities. Some stores may place fresh items on clearance or offer special promotions early in the day to attract morning shoppers. By taking advantage of these deals, you can stretch your grocery budget further and potentially save money on high-quality products that might otherwise be more expensive later in the day.

In essence, choosing the best time for grocery shopping, particularly in the morning, aligns with both practical considerations and personal well-being. It allows you to access fresh and high-quality products, navigate the store with ease, and enjoy a calm and stress-free shopping environment. By prioritizing the early hours for your grocery runs, you can optimize your shopping experience, discover savings opportunities, and set a positive tone for the rest of your day.

# Chapter 7: Do Grocery Shopping Without Kids

Moving around the aisles of a grocery store with children in tow can transform a routine task into a challenging adventure. For many parents, the decision to bring their kids along often results in a slower and more demanding shopping experience. Unlike shopping alone or with a partner, which tends to be efficient and focused, shopping with children requires patience, preparation, and a strategic approach.

One of the primary challenges of grocery shopping with kids is the significant increase in time consumption. What might take an hour alone can easily extend to double or more when children accompany you. Their curiosity, frequent distractions, and inevitable requests for various treats and snacks elongate the shopping process. This extended time in the store not only tests your patience but also your ability to adhere to a shopping list and budget.

Children's fondness for sweets, cookies, and other tempting treats can also impact your grocery bill. While shopping alone might involve sticking strictly to essentials, the presence of children often leads to spontaneous purchases to satisfy their cravings or requests. These items tend to be higher-priced and less nutritious, contributing to both increased spending and potential compromises on health-conscious choices.

Furthermore, shopping with kids can be stressful and distracting. Managing their behavior, addressing their needs, and navigating through crowded aisles while keeping them entertained require constant attention and energy. This distraction can lead to oversights such as forgetting essential items or overlooking details like product quality and expiration dates.

To mitigate these challenges, parents often develop strategies to streamline their grocery shopping experience. Some opt for shopping during quieter times of the day when stores are less crowded, minimizing the sensory overload and distractions for both children and themselves. Planning ahead by creating a shopping list together with the kids, outlining expectations, and setting ground rules can help maintain focus and reduce impulse purchases.

Another approach is to engage children actively in the shopping process by assigning them small tasks, such as selecting fruits or vegetables, or allowing them to choose one special item within a set budget. This involvement not only keeps them occupied but also provides a valuable learning opportunity about food choices, budgeting, and responsibility.

Moreover, leveraging technology like grocery apps that offer online ordering or curbside pickup can be a game-changer for busy parents. This option eliminates the need to navigate through the store altogether, providing convenience and efficiency while minimizing the challenges associated with shopping with kids.

Shopping for groceries without children doesn't mean neglecting their needs; rather, it allows adults to focus on purchasing nutritious, quality, and cost-effective food items that cater to their children's preferences. It enables a peaceful and efficient shopping experience where decisions are made based on value for money and nutritional value rather than impulsive purchases influenced by children's desires that may not align with smart shopping practices. This approach ensures that grocery trips are purposeful, budget-friendly, and conducive to maintaining a healthy eating plan for the entire family.

While grocery shopping with children presents unique challenges, it can also be an opportunity for bonding and learning. By implementing practical strategies and maintaining a positive attitude, parents can conduct this experience more smoothly, ensuring both their grocery needs and their children's well-being are met effectively.

# Chapter 8: Selecting Between Online and In-Store Purchases

A savvy shopper understands the importance of choosing between online purchases and visiting a physical grocery store. This decision isn't just about convenience; it's about optimizing your budget, maximizing efficiency, and enhancing your overall shopping experience. Certain items are more cost-effective to purchase online than in-store. By strategically selecting items online, you not only save money but also reduce the bulk in your shopping cart during physical store visits. This streamlined approach saves valuable time and conserves energy, allowing you to focus on other priorities.

One of the key benefits of buying groceries online is cost-effectiveness. Online platforms often offer discounts, promotions, and subscription services that can significantly lower costs for certain products compared to their in-store counterparts. Non-perishable items, household supplies, and bulk goods are typically more economical to purchase online, benefiting from reduced overhead costs and competitive pricing strategies employed by online retailers. Moreover, online shopping enables you to easily compare prices across different websites, ensuring you get the best deal without the need to physically visit multiple stores.

In addition to cost savings, online grocery shopping offers unparalleled convenience. It allows you to shop from the comfort of your home or office, eliminating the need to navigate crowded aisles or wait in long checkout lines. This convenience is particularly advantageous for busy individuals or families with limited time for traditional grocery runs. Furthermore, online platforms often provide flexible delivery options, including same-day or next-day delivery, which can accommodate varying schedules and preferences.

Despite the benefits of online shopping, visiting a physical grocery store has its own advantages, particularly when it comes to selecting fresh produce, meats, and dairy products. The tactile experience of physically inspecting items ensures you can assess their quality, freshness, and expiration dates firsthand. This is crucial for maintaining dietary preferences, adhering to specific meal plans, or accommodating individual tastes within your household. In-store shopping also allows you to take advantage of immediate needs or last-minute adjustments to your shopping list based on availability and seasonal offerings.

Moreover, shopping in-store provides opportunities to capitalize on in-person promotions, clearance sales, and manager specials that may not be available online. Engaging directly with store staff can also yield valuable recommendations or insights into new products or local favorites. These interactions can enhance your shopping experience and introduce you to items you may not have considered otherwise.

Balancing between online and in-store shopping involves staying informed about price comparisons, product availability, and delivery options. Utilizing grocery apps, price comparison websites, and loyalty programs can help you make informed decisions about where and when to purchase specific items. By adapting your shopping strategy based on these insights, you can maximize savings, efficiency, and satisfaction with each grocery shopping trip.

The choice between online and in-store shopping should be driven by your specific needs, preferences, and circumstances. Online shopping offers convenience, cost savings, and a wide selection of products, particularly for non-perishable items and bulk purchases. On the other hand, in-store shopping allows for a hands-on selection of fresh foods and immediate access to store promotions. By leveraging the strengths of both approaches, you can create a personalized grocery shopping strategy that enhances efficiency and meets your household's needs effectively.

# Chapter 9: Shopping Off-Brand Items

Shopping for off-brand items, often referred to as store brands or generics, is a savvy approach to grocery shopping that can yield significant benefits. These products, while not as widely advertised or recognized as national brands, offer compelling reasons to consider them for your shopping list. It's important to understand why choosing off-brand items can be a smart strategy for budget-conscious and quality-focused shoppers alike.

Off-brand items are typically produced by retailers or manufacturers under their own labels. They often mimic the composition and quality of well-known national brands but are offered at lower prices. This cost-effectiveness stems from reduced marketing and advertising expenses, allowing savings to be passed on to consumers. By opting for off-brand products, shoppers can achieve substantial savings on their grocery bills without sacrificing quality.

Contrary to popular belief, off-brand items frequently match or exceed the quality standards of their national brand counterparts. Many off-brand products are manufactured in the same facilities as their branded equivalents, using similar ingredients and production processes. This ensures that consumers receive comparable quality at a lower cost. Whether it's canned goods, snacks, dairy products, or household essentials like cleaning supplies, off-brand items offer a viable alternative that meets everyday needs without compromising on taste or efficacy.

One of the primary reasons to consider off-brand shopping is the significant cost savings it provides. On average, off-brand products can be priced 15% to 30% lower than national brands. This pricing advantage extends across various product categories, allowing shoppers to stretch their grocery budgets further. For families and individuals looking to reduce household expenses without sacrificing the quality of their purchases, opting for off-brand items can make a substantial difference over time.

Today's grocery shelves boast a wide array of off-brand options, ranging from basic staples to specialized products. Retailers and grocery chains have expanded their off-brand offerings to include organic, gluten-free, and gourmet items, catering to diverse consumer preferences. This variety not only enhances choice but also allows shoppers to explore new products and flavors without breaking the bank. Whether you're stocking up on pantry essentials or trying out a new snack, off-brand selections offer versatility and affordability.

Choosing off-brand items can also align with environmentally conscious shopping practices. Many off-brand products emphasize sustainable sourcing, reduced packaging waste, and ethical manufacturing practices. By supporting retailers' private label initiatives or opting for generics, consumers contribute to reducing carbon footprints and promoting responsible consumption. This aspect resonates with shoppers who prioritize environmental stewardship in their purchasing decisions.

As off-brand items gain popularity and consumer trust, retailers continue to invest in improving their product offerings. This includes enhancing packaging, nutritional value, and taste profiles to meet evolving consumer expectations. Grocery stores often offer satisfaction guarantees or refund policies on their off-brand products, providing peace of mind to shoppers who are trying new items or brands for the first time.

Incorporating off-brand items into your shopping strategy involves a few practical steps. Start by identifying product categories where cost savings are significant and quality is consistent. Compare prices per unit or ounce between off-brand and national-brand options to gauge savings accurately. Experiment with different off-brand products over time to determine which ones best meet your family's preferences and nutritional needs.

Shopping for off-brand items is a strategic and economical choice that empowers consumers to make informed decisions about their grocery purchases. By leveraging the affordability, quality, and variety offered by off-brand products, shoppers can effectively manage their budgets while enjoying comparable products to national brands. Whether you're looking to reduce grocery expenses, explore new flavors, or support sustainable practices, off-brand shopping offers a practical solution that aligns with the principles of clever grocery shopping.

# Chapter 10: Maximizing Savings with Digital Tools

In today's era of rapid digital advancement and easy access to information, leveraging digital tools is not just convenient but essential for savvy grocery shoppers looking to maximize their savings. There are three powerful strategies—using coupons effectively, utilizing rebate apps for cashback, and leveraging points and loyalty programs—that harness the power of technology to stretch your grocery budget further.

Coupons have evolved from paper clippings to digital codes accessible through websites and mobile apps. They offer instant discounts on a variety of products, helping shoppers save money without compromising on quality. Smart shoppers strategically plan their purchases around available coupons, taking advantage of store policies that allow stacking coupons with sales for maximum savings. By staying informed about promotional periods and coupon expiration dates, shoppers can optimize their grocery spending and reduce their overall costs significantly.

Rebate apps represent a modern approach to saving money after shopping. There are so many apps to choose from that offer cash back incentives for scanning receipts or purchasing specific items. These apps make earning money back on everyday purchases effortless, encouraging users to upload receipts and redeem offers conveniently from their smartphones. By regularly checking for new deals and optimizing their shopping lists based on available rebates, shoppers can accumulate substantial cashback over time, effectively lowering their grocery expenses.

Grocery stores and chains incentivize customer loyalty through points-based programs that reward regular shoppers with discounts, personalized offers, and redeemable points. By signing up for these programs and using associated cards or apps during checkout, shoppers earn points on purchases that can later be redeemed for groceries or other merchandise. Loyalty programs not only enhance the shopping experience by providing exclusive benefits but also encourage repeat business through targeted promotions tailored to individual shopping preferences.

The true power of these digital tools lies in their integration and strategic use. Savvy shoppers can combine coupons with rebate app offers and loyalty program rewards to maximize their savings on each shopping trip. This synergistic approach allows consumers to stretch their grocery budget further while enjoying the convenience of digital shopping aids. Understanding how these tools complement each other empowers shoppers to make informed decisions, capitalize on available discounts, and achieve financial goals without compromising on quality or choice.

 Indeed, digital tools offer unparalleled opportunities to save money and enhance shopping experiences. Taking advantage of these resources is not just practical but also advantageous. By making use of coupons, rebate apps, and loyalty programs, shoppers can navigate the complexities of grocery shopping with ease, capitalize on available discounts, and optimize their spending habits effectively. Whether shopping online or in-store, integrating digital tools into your shopping routine ensures that every purchase contributes to greater savings and a more fulfilling shopping experience.

# Chapter 11: Maximizing Savings with Bulk Purchases

Bulk purchasing is a savvy approach to saving money on essential grocery items with longer shelf lives. By purchasing these items at discounted bulk prices, you ensure significant savings over time while maintaining the convenience of having a well-stocked pantry. Bulk buying fits with your household's needs and budget, and you'll reap the benefits of both financial prudence and sustainable living. Using the opportunity of bulk purchasing optimizes your grocery spending and ensures that your household remains well-prepared for everyday needs without overspending. Bulk shopping for items helps maximize savings, ensuring you save money without compromising on quality or convenience.

When it comes to everyday essentials like toilet paper, washing powder, bath gels, and long-shelf-life food items such as legumes and cooking oil, buying in bulk can significantly reduce your overall grocery expenses. By purchasing these items in larger quantities, you benefit from lower per-unit costs, making it a cost-effective solution for managing your household budget. This approach not only saves you money in the long run but also reduces the frequency of shopping trips, freeing up your time for other activities.

Bulk buying is all about maximizing cost-effectiveness. Whether you're stocking up for a large family or simply want to avoid running out of essential items, buying in bulk ensures that you get the most value for your money. The upfront investment in larger quantities pays off by reducing the unit cost of each item, allowing you to allocate your grocery budget more efficiently.

One of the primary benefits of buying in bulk is the convenience it provides. By purchasing larger quantities of regularly used items, you minimize the need for frequent trips to the store or repeated online orders. This not only saves you time but also ensures that you always have a sufficient supply of essentials at home. It's a practical solution that fits seamlessly into busy lifestyles, allowing you to focus on what matters most without worrying about running out of everyday necessities.

In addition to financial savings and convenience, bulk buying can also have environmental benefits. By reducing packaging waste and minimizing transportation emissions associated with frequent shopping trips, bulk purchasing supports sustainable consumption practices. Choosing bulk options for products with longer shelf life helps reduce overall environmental impact, making it a responsible choice for eco-conscious shoppers.

To make the most of bulk purchases, it's essential to plan strategically. Start by evaluating your household's consumption patterns and identifying which items are suitable for bulk buying based on their shelf life and usage frequency. Research reputable suppliers or retailers known for their quality products and competitive pricing. Consider investing in proper storage solutions to maintain the freshness and usability of bulk-bought items over time.

Whether you're stocking up for a large family or simply want to streamline your grocery shopping routine, buying discounted items in bulk offers practical benefits that align with both financial prudence and responsible consumption practices. By making the best of cheap bulk purchases, you make your grocery budget work harder for you while ensuring that your household always stays well-stocked with the essentials.

# Chapter 12. Avoiding Impulse Buys

Avoiding impulse buys is crucial for maintaining a balanced budget and making thoughtful purchasing decisions. Many people fall into the trap of spontaneous purchases, which can lead to overspending and accumulating items that aren't truly needed. Understanding how to avoid impulse buys involves recognizing triggers, planning ahead, and adopting mindful shopping habits.

Avoiding impulse buys requires mindfulness, planning, and self-discipline. By understanding your triggers, setting clear intentions, and being mindful of your emotions, you can cultivate healthier shopping habits that prioritize long-term financial goals and reduce unnecessary spending.

One effective strategy is never to shop for anything without a plan. Only stick to your shopping list. because that helps you minimize the temptation to make impulse purchases based on fleeting desires or advertisements. Another helpful approach is to set a budget for each shopping trip and allocate specific amounts for different categories. This budgeting technique helps prioritize needs over wants and encourages responsible spending. By knowing how much you intend to spend overall, you can resist the urge to splurge on unnecessary items that catch your eye.

Avoiding impulse buys also involves being mindful of your emotions and the shopping environment. Stress, boredom, or peer influence can all contribute to impulse buying tendencies. Taking a moment to pause and reflect on whether a purchase is truly necessary can help you make more informed decisions and avoid regretful spending.

Furthermore, consider implementing a waiting period before making non-essential purchases. This could involve waiting 24 hours or longer before revisiting the decision to buy an item. Often, this delay allows time to evaluate whether the purchase is truly needed or if it was driven by impulse.

Online shopping presents unique challenges when it comes to impulse buys. One way to mitigate this is by removing saved payment information from websites and apps. This extra step during checkout can serve as a reminder to reassess the purchase and ensure it aligns with your budget and needs.

Shopping with a friend or family member who can provide objective feedback can also help curb impulse buys. They can offer a different perspective and encourage you to stick to your planned purchases, making the shopping experience more intentional and less driven by spontaneous urges.

Lastly, practicing gratitude for what you already have can shift focus away from the desire for new possessions. By appreciating the items you own and their value, you may find yourself less inclined to make impulse purchases simply to acquire more. Avoiding impulse buys requires mindfulness, planning, and self-discipline. By understanding your triggers, setting clear intentions, and being mindful of your emotions, you can cultivate healthier shopping habits that prioritize long-term financial goals and reduce unnecessary spending.

# Chapter 13: Freezing Fresh Produce for Long-Term Savings

Taking advantage of seasonal abundance is a savvy way to save money on groceries, particularly when it comes to fresh produce like tomatoes, onions, garlic, and other fruits and vegetables that are plentiful during certain times of the year. You can easily make the most of seasonal bargains by freezing fresh produce for extended use, ensuring high quality, and enjoying tasty frozen food that saves you time.

When fruits and vegetables are in season, their prices often drop due to increased supply. Farmers and grocery stores offer discounts to move surplus stock, making it an ideal time to stock up on your favorite produce items without breaking the bank. Seasonal produce is not only more affordable but also tends to be at its peak freshness and flavor, making it a nutritious choice for your meals.

Once you've purchased your seasonal produce haul, it's time to prepare it for freezing. Start by washing the fruits and vegetables thoroughly to remove any dirt or pesticides. For items like tomatoes, blanching (briefly boiling and then plunging into ice water) can help preserve color and texture before freezing, ensuring they retain their delicious taste and nutrients.

Packaging plays a crucial role in maintaining the quality of frozen produce. Opt for freezer-safe plastic bags or airtight plastic containers. Remove excess air from the bags before sealing to prevent freezer burn, and label each package with the contents and date of freezing for easy identification later.

Spread fruits, like berries or sliced bananas, on a baking sheet in a single layer before freezing. Once frozen, transfer them to bags for easier portioning and storage. Vegetables can be frozen as whole pieces, slices, or dice, depending on how you plan to use them later. This method not only extends their shelf life but also saves money compared to purchasing frozen items from the store, allowing you to control portion sizes and avoid added preservatives or excess salt.

Rotate your frozen produce to use older items first, and experiment with recipes that incorporate frozen fruits and vegetables into smoothies, soups, stews, and casseroles. By doing so, you can enjoy nutritious meals year-round while minimizing food waste and maximizing savings. Proper preparation and storage ensure your freezer is stocked with wholesome ingredients ready to elevate your culinary creations without compromising on quality or budget.

By taking advantage of seasonal bargains and freezing fresh produce, you can enjoy nutritious meals year-round while minimizing food waste and maximizing savings. With proper preparation and storage, you'll have a freezer stocked with wholesome ingredients ready to elevate your culinary creations without compromising on quality or budget.

# Chapter 14: Ask Others for Information

One of the most valuable strategies for savvy grocery shopping is tapping into the wealth of information shared by others. Whether it's through friends, colleagues, neighbors, or coworkers, gathering insights and tips can lead to discovering great deals, new products, and efficient shopping strategies.

When you engage with others, you often gain access to timely information that might not be readily available elsewhere. For instance, someone in your social circle might have recently discovered a local market with significantly lower prices on certain items or could inform you about ongoing promotions at nearby stores that offer substantial savings.

Beyond just finding good deals, discussing grocery shopping with others can provide valuable insights into different approaches and methods. You can learn how others manage their grocery budgets, organize shopping trips, and plan meals effectively. This exchange of ideas can inspire new strategies to optimize your own grocery shopping routine, potentially saving both time and money.

Friends and colleagues can also offer firsthand experiences with specific products, helping you make informed decisions about what to buy. They might recommend brands that offer better quality or better value for money, or they might caution you about products that don't meet their expectations, saving you from potential disappointment.

Moreover, engaging in conversations about grocery-related matters allows you to benefit from collective wisdom and diverse perspectives. Different individuals may have unique dietary preferences, cooking styles, or cultural influences that shape their grocery choices. By learning from these differences, you can broaden your culinary horizons and discover new ingredients or recipes to try, enhancing your overall cooking and eating experiences.

Practical tips and life hacks often emerge from casual conversations about grocery shopping. Whether it's a time-saving trick for meal preparation, a storage solution that extends the shelf life of perishable items, or a creative way to use leftovers, these insights can significantly improve your grocery shopping experience.

In essence, don't underestimate the power of asking others for information when it comes to grocery shopping. Engaging in conversations, seeking recommendations, and sharing experiences can lead to discovering hidden gems, saving money, and improving your overall shopping efficiency. By leveraging the collective knowledge of your social network, you can navigate the grocery aisles with confidence and maximize the value of every shopping trip.

# Chapter 15. Benefits of Buying Frozen Produce

Frozen produce offers a range of advantages that cater to both practicality and nutrition-conscious shoppers. Choosing frozen fruits and vegetables is not just about convenience; it's a strategic decision that can enhance meal planning efficiency, nutritional intake, financial savings, and even contribute to sustainability efforts. Let's delve into the myriad benefits of incorporating frozen produce into your grocery shopping routine.

One of the foremost benefits of frozen produce is its unmatched convenience. Available year-round and often pre-prepared, frozen fruits and vegetables streamline meal preparation, saving valuable time and effort. Whether you're preparing a quick weekday dinner or a batch of smoothies, having readily accessible frozen ingredients eliminates the need for washing, peeling, or chopping, which can be time-consuming with fresh produce.

Moreover, frozen produce eliminates the seasonal limitations that fresh produce often entails. You can enjoy your favorite fruits and vegetables regardless of the time of year, ensuring a consistent supply of ingredients for your culinary creations. This accessibility is particularly beneficial for individuals with busy lifestyles or those living in areas where fresh produce variety might be limited.

Contrary to common misconceptions, frozen produce can be just as nutritious, if not more so, than fresh produce. The rapid freezing techniques employed by manufacturers lock in essential vitamins and minerals at their peak freshness. In contrast, fresh produce may lose some of its nutritional value during prolonged storage and transportation from farm to store.

Research has shown that certain nutrients, such as vitamin C and antioxidants, are well-preserved in frozen fruits and vegetables. This makes frozen options an excellent choice for maintaining a balanced diet year-round, providing a reliable source of key nutrients without compromising on quality.

Opting for frozen produce can also be a prudent financial decision. While the upfront cost per pound of frozen produce may sometimes be slightly higher than fresh, the extended shelf life of frozen items helps minimize waste. Fresh produce, on the other hand, is more susceptible to spoilage, often leading to discarded fruits and vegetables that contribute to higher grocery expenses over time.

By reducing food waste and maximizing the usability of each purchase, frozen produce allows consumers to stretch their grocery budgets further. Additionally, purchasing frozen produce in bulk or during sales can yield significant savings, making it an economical choice for households looking to balance nutrition and financial stewardship.

From an environmental standpoint, frozen produce can contribute to sustainability efforts in several ways. By reducing food waste through extended shelf life, frozen options help minimize the carbon footprint associated with discarded food. Furthermore, frozen produce often undergoes efficient transportation methods, reducing overall energy consumption and greenhouse gas emissions compared to transporting perishable fresh produce over long distances.

Choosing locally-produced frozen produce further enhances sustainability by supporting regional agriculture and reducing the environmental impact of transportation. Additionally, some frozen produce brands are committed to sustainable farming practices and packaging, further mitigating their environmental footprint.

Frozen produce offers versatility in culinary applications. Beyond their traditional uses in smoothies and soups, frozen fruits can be thawed and incorporated into desserts, yogurt parfaits, and baked goods. Frozen vegetables are ideal for stir-fries, casseroles, and side dishes, providing convenience without sacrificing nutritional value or flavor.

The availability of pre-cut and pre-packaged frozen produce also simplifies portion control and meal planning. It allows households to prepare meals quickly without compromising on healthfulness or taste, making it easier to maintain a balanced diet amidst busy schedules.

Frozen produce undergoes stringent quality control measures to ensure safety and freshness. From harvesting to freezing, manufacturers adhere to strict guidelines to preserve the integrity of the produce. This includes rapid freezing techniques that maintain texture and flavor while minimizing the formation of ice crystals that can affect taste and consistency.

Furthermore, frozen produce is often free from additives or preservatives, particularly when opting for plain frozen fruits and vegetables without sauces or seasonings. This purity ensures that consumers can enjoy natural flavors and nutritional benefits without unnecessary ingredients.

Therefore, the benefits of buying frozen produce extend far beyond mere convenience. It encompasses nutritional integrity, financial savings, environmental sustainability, culinary versatility, and quality assurance. By incorporating frozen fruits and vegetables into your shopping routine, you can enhance meal planning efficiency, support a balanced diet, and contribute to sustainable consumption practices.

Whether you're a busy professional seeking convenient meal solutions, a budget-conscious shopper looking to reduce food waste, or an environmentally conscious consumer aiming to minimize your carbon footprint, frozen produce offers a practical and beneficial choice. Embrace the versatility and nutritional benefits of frozen options to elevate your grocery shopping experience and enjoy the convenience of having wholesome ingredients readily available for your everyday meals.

# Chapter 16. Make Arrangements for Quick Meals

Making arrangements for quick meal preparation at home involves strategic planning and thoughtful grocery shopping to ensure you're prepared for various situations that may arise. Whether it's unexpected guests, busy schedules, a lack of cooking motivation, or times when you're not feeling up to preparing elaborate meals, having a well-stocked pantry can be a lifesaver.

One essential aspect of preparing for quick meals is stocking up on versatile and convenient ingredients. Canned foods such as beans, tomatoes, soups, and tuna provide a quick and easy base for many dishes. They can be incorporated into soups, stews, pasta sauces, or used as toppings for pizzas and salads. These items have a long shelf life and are readily available, making them ideal for emergencies or when time is short.

Frozen items also play a crucial role in quick meal preparation. Frozen vegetables, fruits, pre-cooked meats, and seafood retain their nutrients well and require minimal preparation. They can be quickly thawed and added to stir-fries, casseroles, or simply steamed as a side dish. Frozen pizzas, chicken nuggets, and other prepared foods offer convenience without sacrificing taste or nutrition, making them perfect for busy weeknights or unexpected dinner guests.

Ready-to-eat meals are another valuable addition to your pantry. These include microwavable dinners, pre-packaged salads, sandwiches, and wraps that require little to no preparation. They are ideal for those days when cooking from scratch is not feasible or when you need a quick meal solution on the go. Ready-to-eat meals come in a variety of options to suit different dietary preferences and can be a convenient way to ensure you have a balanced meal without spending hours in the kitchen.

In addition to these prepared foods, staples like bread and eggs provide versatility in meal planning. Bread can be used for sandwiches, toast with various toppings, or as a base for quick pizzas or bruschetta. Eggs can be scrambled, fried, or turned into omelets for a quick and satisfying breakfast, lunch, or dinner option.

Strategically planning your grocery shopping involves anticipating your needs based on your weekly schedule and potential disruptions. It's essential to stock up on items that align with your dietary preferences and nutritional needs while ensuring freshness and minimizing waste. Regularly rotating your stock and checking expiration dates can help maintain a well-organized pantry and ensure you're always prepared for any situation that may arise.

By adopting a proactive approach to meal preparation and grocery shopping, you empower yourself to handle daily challenges with ease and maintain a healthy and balanced diet. Whether it's enjoying a quick dinner after a long day at work or hosting unexpected guests without stress, preparing for quick meal solutions at home allows you to prioritize convenience, nutrition, and overall well-being in your everyday life.

# Chapter 17. The Importance of Keeping Receipts

When shopping at grocery stores, keeping your receipts is crucial for several reasons. Firstly, receipts serve as concrete proof of your purchase. They detail essential information such as the date and time of purchase, item descriptions, prices paid, any discounts applied, and the method of payment used. This documentation is essential for verifying that the items being returned or exchanged were bought from that specific store, ensuring compliance with their return policies, and facilitating a smooth transaction process.

In cases where a purchased grocery item turns out to be defective, damaged, expired, or doesn't meet your expectations, having the original receipt is essential. It acts as your documented proof of purchase and validates your entitlement to seek resolution. Without a receipt, some stores may be hesitant or unable to process returns or exchanges, potentially leaving you without recourse. Many grocery retailers have strict policies requiring receipts for returns, and without one, you may only be eligible for store credit or an exchange at the current selling price.

Moreover, receipts play a crucial role in managing household budgets and tracking expenses. By retaining your grocery receipts, you can accurately monitor your spending patterns, identify any discrepancies, and plan future purchases accordingly. This financial record-keeping helps you stay within your budget and make informed decisions about your grocery shopping habits.

Organizing your grocery receipts in a designated folder or using digital receipt-tracking methods can further streamline your record-keeping process. Digital receipts, often available through email or mobile apps provided by grocery stores, offer a convenient and environmentally friendly alternative to paper receipts. Storing digital copies on your smartphone or computer ensures that your proof of purchase is always accessible, reducing the risk of losing or misplacing important documents.

For larger grocery purchases or items with extended warranties, retaining the original receipt becomes even more critical. It acts as a safeguard against unforeseen issues that may arise, such as discovering a defect in a kitchen appliance or encountering spoiled perishable goods shortly after purchase. Having the receipt readily available can expedite resolution with the store's customer service department, ensuring that you receive appropriate compensation or a replacement product without unnecessary delays.

Maintaining the practice of keeping grocery receipts is not just about organization; it's about protecting your consumer rights and ensuring a seamless shopping experience. It empowers you to assert your entitlement to returns, exchanges, or refunds when necessary, provides a financial record for budgeting purposes, and supports effective management of household expenses. By adopting good receipt management habits, you enhance your ability to resolve any issues that may arise with grocery purchases promptly and satisfactorily.

# Chapter 18. Seasonal Grocery Planning for Absences

Tailoring your grocery shopping habits to seasonal needs involves adjusting your purchases based on upcoming holidays, vacations, or temporary absences from home. This strategic approach ensures that you have the right amount and type of food on hand, minimizing waste and optimizing convenience during your absence.

When preparing for holidays or extended vacations, thoughtful grocery planning becomes crucial to avoid purchasing perishable items that may spoil before your return. Consider the duration of your absence and the availability of dining options at your destination to make informed decisions about what groceries to buy and what to leave off your shopping list.

One of the primary reasons for tailoring your grocery shopping to seasonal needs is to prevent food waste. Planning meals in advance is essential for using up perishable items first and incorporating non-perishable alternatives for later meals. Utilize frozen fruits and vegetables, canned goods, pasta, rice, and other shelf-stable items to extend the freshness of your meals and minimize the likelihood of food spoilage during your absence.

Financially, adapting your grocery shopping habits to seasonal needs also leads to savings. By avoiding unnecessary purchases of perishable items that won't be consumed during your absence, you can optimize your grocery budget. Allocate funds towards items with longer shelf lives or ingredients more suitable for meals before you leave, ensuring efficient use of your resources.

Enhancing convenience and reducing stress is another benefit of tailoring your grocery shopping to seasonal needs. Stock up on essentials and non-perishable items that can be easily stored and used upon your return. This preparation ensures that you have quick and convenient meal options available without the need for immediate shopping trips, allowing for a smoother transition back into your daily routine after your absence.

When planning for seasonal absences, consider the dining options and availability of grocery stores at your destination if you are traveling. Research local options to determine what essentials you might need to bring with you and what you can purchase upon arrival. Monitoring expiration dates on items you plan to leave behind helps maintain their freshness and quality until your return, minimizing the risk of waste and ensuring you have usable supplies on hand.

Communicate with household members or roommates if others will be staying at home while you're away. Coordinate meal plans and grocery needs to ensure everyone is aware of what's available and what needs to be replenished. This collaboration minimizes the risk of overstocking or understocking groceries and promotes efficient use of household resources during your absence.

By integrating these tips into your seasonal grocery planning, you can effectively manage your food supply, maintain financial discipline, and ensure a seamless experience during your time away from home. Embrace these strategies to enhance your overall grocery shopping efficiency and maximize the convenience of managing your household.

# Chapter 19. Smart Beverage Choices to Save Money

Making smart beverage choices can lead to considerable financial benefits, especially when focusing on purchasing large-sized items such as milk, mineral water, juices, fruit syrups, and other drinks. Buying these beverages in bulk or in larger sizes not only saves money but also enhances convenience and reduces the environmental impact. Enjoy the convenience of having beverages readily available at home. Make use of smart beverage choices to not only save money but also support sustainable consumption practices and enhance your overall grocery shopping experience.

Opting for larger containers of milk allows you to capitalize on lower unit prices compared to smaller packages. This approach is particularly cost-effective and versatile, as it enables you to use milk for various homemade dairy products such as cream, yogurt, cheese, and butter. By purchasing in bulk, you not only save money on these essential dairy items but also minimize the frequency of grocery trips, enhancing overall efficiency.

Choosing large-sized mineral water bottles can be economical, especially if your household prefers bottled water vs tap water for convenience or taste reasons. Purchasing larger packs reduces the cost per liter or bottle, making it a practical choice for regular consumers of mineral water. Additionally, reusing mineral water bottles for storing tap water or homemade beverages extends their utility and reduces waste, contributing to environmental sustainability.

Buying juices and fruit syrups in larger containers or multipacks presents significant opportunities for savings. Bulk purchasing allows you to benefit from lower per-unit prices and ensures that you have a supply of refreshing drinks on hand without frequent store visits. This approach not only saves money but also provides convenience, particularly during gatherings or when you need beverages readily available for guests.

Creating your own beverages at home using bulk-purchased ingredients can further contribute to savings. For example, using fruit syrups or concentrates to make homemade sodas or flavored drinks is often more economical than purchasing pre-packaged beverages. It allows you to control ingredients, adjust sweetness levels, and customize flavors to your liking while minimizing packaging waste and reducing overall costs.

Making smart beverage choices by opting for large-sized containers or bulk purchases can significantly reduce your grocery expenses over time. Whether you're stocking up on milk for versatile dairy products, ensuring hydration with economical mineral water choices, or enjoying savings on juices and syrups for everyday refreshments, purchasing in larger quantities ensures lower costs per unit and enhances overall financial efficiency in your household budget.

# Chapter 20. Combining Foods for Savings

Combining food items strategically to maximize value for money while ensuring delicious and nutritious meals is always helpful. By pairing different types of meat with affordable ingredients like potatoes or seasonal vegetables and utilizing cost-effective options available during specific times of the year, you can achieve both economic savings and culinary satisfaction.

One effective strategy is to incorporate versatile ingredients, such as potatoes, into dishes featuring meats like chicken or beef. Potatoes are budget-friendly and can enhance the volume and nutritional content of meals without compromising on taste. For example, preparing hearty stews or casseroles with chicken and potatoes not only stretches your budget but also creates satisfying meals that can be enjoyed over several servings.

Another approach is to capitalize on seasonal produce or vegetables that are more affordable during certain times of the year. By combining these vegetables with meats like beef or poultry, you can create balanced and flavorful dishes such as vegetable-beef stir-fry or chicken and vegetable skewers. This not only helps in managing costs but also adds variety and freshness to your diet based on what is readily available and economical.

Incorporating legumes, such as beans or lentils, with ground meats is another economical and nutritious option. Legumes are rich in protein and fiber, making them excellent companions to beef or ground meat in dishes like chili con carne or meatballs with lentil sauce. This combination not only adds texture and flavor but also boosts the nutritional value of the meal while keeping costs down.

Salads provide a versatile canvas for combining affordable fresh vegetables with a variety of proteins or grains. By mixing inexpensive leafy greens and seasonal vegetables with grilled chicken, canned tuna, or boiled eggs, you can create satisfying and nutrient-rich salads that serve as main courses or hearty sides. Dressing salads with homemade vinaigrettes or simple oil and vinegar combinations further enhances flavor without breaking the budget.

Furthermore, exploring global cuisines can inspire creative combinations that are both economical and delicious. Dishes like vegetable and meat risottos, stir-fried noodles with mixed vegetables and shrimp, or bean-based soups with affordable cuts of pork or chicken showcase how diverse ingredients can be harmoniously combined to create satisfying meals.

Mastering the art of combining food items to create value meals involves strategic planning and creativity. By integrating affordable staples like potatoes, seasonal vegetables, legumes, and versatile proteins, you can achieve savings while enhancing the nutritional quality and flavor of your meals. Whether you're cooking for yourself, your family, or entertaining guests, these cost-effective and delicious combinations ensure that every meal is a delightful balance of economy, health, and taste.

# Chapter 21. Economical Homemade Delights

By preparing food items at home using inexpensive ingredients, taking advantage of seasonal price variations, and highlighting items that are significantly cheaper to make yourself than to purchase pre-made from grocery stores, These homemade creations not only save money but also allow for customization, freshness, and control over ingredients, ensuring healthier and tastier meals.

Let's begin with preserving seasonal vegetables. During the summer, when vegetables like cucumbers are plentiful and affordable, making homemade pickles is a cost-effective option. By purchasing cucumbers in bulk when prices are low, you can create pickles with your preferred flavors and spices, adjusting sweetness and acidity levels to suit your taste.

Bread is another staple that can be much cheaper to make at home than to buy from a store, especially when considering specialty or artisanal varieties. With basic ingredients like flour, yeast, water, and salt, you can create fresh, fragrant loaves of bread tailored to your preferences. Homemade bread not only saves money but also ensures you know exactly what goes into each loaf, avoiding unnecessary additives or preservatives.

For those seeking dairy alternatives, making oat milk at home is a budget-friendly option. Oats are affordable and readily available, and blending them with water and straining yields a creamy, nutritious milk alternative. This DIY approach not only saves on packaging and transportation costs associated with store-bought alternatives but also allows for customization in sweetness and flavoring.

Using an air fryer to prepare chicken wings is another economical choice compared to purchasing pre-cooked wings. Air-frying requires minimal oil and produces crispy wings with less fat, making it a healthier and more budget-conscious option for enjoying this popular dish at home.

When tomatoes are abundant and inexpensive in the summer months at grocery stores, making homemade ketchup or spaghetti sauce is both economical and flavorful. By simmering fresh tomatoes with herbs, spices, and a touch of sweetness, you can create sauces that rival store-bought versions in taste while controlling the quality and quantity of ingredients used.

For breakfast favorites, homemade pancakes are not only a cost-effective choice but also allow for creativity in flavor combinations and toppings. Basic ingredients like flour, eggs, milk, and baking powder can be transformed into fluffy pancakes that are perfect for any meal of the day.

Salad dressings are another area where homemade versions excel in taste and cost efficiency. By mixing simple ingredients like olive oil, vinegar, herbs, and spices, you can create a variety of dressings that elevate salads and other dishes while avoiding the added sugars and preservatives often found in store-bought options.

Taking advantage of seasonal fruit sales, such as bananas, to make homemade milkshakes is a refreshing and budget-friendly treat. Blending ripe bananas with milk or yogurt and a dash of flavorings like cocoa powder or vanilla extract results in creamy milkshakes that are both nutritious and satisfying.

Finally, preparing meat broth at home using leftover bones or inexpensive cuts of meat is a thrifty way to enhance soups, stews, and sauces. Simmering bones or meat with vegetables and herbs extracts rich flavors and nutrients, creating a base that is far superior in taste and quality to store-bought broths or bouillons.

Mastering the art of making food items from cheap ingredients at home not only saves money but also allows for greater control over ingredients, customization to personal preferences, and the satisfaction of creating wholesome meals from scratch. Whether you're preserving seasonal produce, baking bread, crafting dairy alternatives, or preparing sauces and meals, these homemade delights showcase the practicality and creativity of home cooking while enhancing overall health and taste.

# Chapter 22. Check Expiration Dates

It's important to check expiration dates when shopping for groceries. By selecting items with the longest expiration dates, you ensure freshness and maximize the quality of the products you bring home. This practice not only contributes to better-tasting meals but also minimizes the risk of wasting money on items that may spoil before you have a chance to use them.

When browsing through grocery aisles, it's essential to prioritize items with longer expiration dates. Products with extended shelf lives are typically freshly manufactured or processed, indicating that they were recently produced and are less likely to have deteriorated in quality. This is particularly crucial for perishable items like dairy products, eggs, desserts, and fresh produce, where freshness directly impacts taste and nutritional value.

Avoiding items that are nearing their expiration dates is also key. Products approaching their expiration may not only have diminished freshness but also pose a higher risk of spoilage or reduced efficacy, especially for items like medications or skincare products where effectiveness is critical. By opting for products with longer expiration dates, you can confidently use them within their optimal period, ensuring maximum enjoyment and utility.

Furthermore, it's prudent to inspect multiple samples of the same product, particularly for items like canned goods or packaged foods where batches may vary. Even within the same brand and product category, different batches can have varying expiration dates, reflecting differences in manufacturing or distribution timelines. By comparing expiration dates across samples, you increase the likelihood of selecting the freshest and highest-quality options available.

Pay special attention to perishable items such as seafood, meats, and ready-to-eat meals, where expiration dates can vary widely based on factors like processing date and storage conditions. Choosing products with the longest expiration dates helps minimize the risk of purchasing items that may have been sitting on shelves longer, ensuring they maintain their optimal flavor and texture.

Checking expiration dates when shopping for groceries is essential for ensuring freshness, quality, and value for money. By selecting products with the longest expiration dates, you prioritize freshness and reduce the risk of purchasing items that may not meet your expectations. Whether you're shopping for dairy products, packaged goods, or fresh produce, this practice empowers you to make informed choices that enhance the overall enjoyment and satisfaction of your grocery shopping experience.

# Chapter 23. Tips for Selecting Fresh Produce

Always choose fresh produce carefully when grocery shopping. While a grocery store may offer a variety of fruits and vegetables, not all items may be of equal quality. It's essential to discern between fresh and less desirable options to avoid purchasing items that may spoil quickly or fail to meet your expectations.

When selecting fruits, it's advantageous to choose specimens that are neither overly ripe nor underripe. Overly ripe fruits are prone to spoilage and may not last long once you bring them home. Conversely, underripe fruits may lack sweetness and require additional time to ripen properly. Opting for fruits that are medium-ripe ensures they are ready to eat soon after purchase and can be enjoyed without the risk of spoilage before consumption.

Similarly, when choosing vegetables, aim for those that are medium-mature. Avoid overly large vegetables, such as tomatoes or onions, as they may have tougher textures or larger, less desirable seeds. For instance, eggplants can develop hard seeds when they are too mature, negatively impacting their taste and texture. Selecting a mix of ripe and slightly less ripe vegetables, such as tomatoes, allows you to enjoy them throughout the week as they continue to ripen naturally.

It's beneficial to inspect each piece of produce carefully, considering factors such as color, texture, and firmness. Quality produce should exhibit vibrant colors, firm textures, and minimal blemishes or bruises. When possible, smell the produce to detect any off-putting odors, which can indicate spoilage.

If you find that certain items in the fruit and vegetable section of a particular grocery store do not meet your standards for freshness or quality, don't hesitate to explore other nearby stores for better options. Shopping around can ensure you find the freshest produce available, minimizing food waste and maximizing the value of your purchases.

So choosing fresh produce involves careful consideration and inspection to ensure optimal quality and longevity. By selecting fruits and vegetables that are medium-ripe and free from defects, you can enjoy nutritious and flavorful meals while minimizing the risk of premature spoilage. This mindful approach not only enhances the quality of your meals but also contributes to reducing food waste and making economic choices in your grocery shopping routine.

# Chapter 24. Tips for Selecting Good-Quality Meat

For those who like eating meat, there are various types of meat available in grocery stores and butcher shops, like beef, chicken, seafood, lamb, minced meat, and more, to ensure that each is chosen with care to guarantee freshness, flavor, and quality.

When selecting beef, look for cuts that are bright red with a firm texture and marbling of fat throughout. Marbling enhances flavor and tenderness. Avoid meat that appears brownish or has a slimy texture, which could indicate spoilage. Steaks and roasts should have a fresh, meaty smell without any off odors.

Choose chicken that has a plump, moist appearance with smooth, unbroken skin. The flesh should feel firm to the touch. Avoid chicken with a slimy or sticky texture, as this can indicate bacterial growth. Check for any unpleasant odors, which may suggest the meat is no longer fresh. Whole chickens and chicken parts should be refrigerated or displayed on ice to maintain freshness.

For seafood, such as fish and shellfish, freshness is paramount. Look for clear, bright eyes on whole fish and firm, shiny flesh that springs back when pressed lightly. Avoid fish with dull, sunken eyes or discolored gills. Shellfish should have tightly closed shells or close when tapped, indicating they are still alive. Fish filets and shellfish should not have a strong fishy odor but rather a clean, briny scent.

Lamb should have a pinkish-red color with white marbling. The meat should have a firm and springy texture when touched. Avoid lamb that appears dark red or has a sticky texture, signs of aging, or improper storage. Fresh lamb has a mild, slightly sweet aroma.

For other meats, take them well if they are really looking fresh and have no bad smell.

When choosing minced meat, look for a bright red color with little to no discoloration. The meat should be finely ground and evenly textured, without excessive liquid or clumps. Avoid minced meat that is brownish or has an unpleasant odor, indicating oxidation or spoilage. Packaged minced meat should be cold to the touch and well-sealed to maintain freshness.

Regardless of the type of meat, there are universal signs of freshness to observe. Fresh meat should have a clean, meaty smell without any odors. It should feel firm and resilient to the touch, indicating it hasn't been sitting around too long. The packaging should be intact and free of leaks or tears, ensuring the meat is protected from contamination and air exposure.

When shopping for meat, visit reputable butchers or grocery stores known for their high-quality products and proper handling practices. Ask the butcher for recommendations or guidance on selecting the best cuts for your needs. Consider the intended use of the meat—whether for grilling, roasting, stewing, or other cooking methods—and choose cuts accordingly.

Mastering the art of meat selection involves careful observation and consideration of each type's unique characteristics. By choosing fresh, high-quality meat, you can ensure delicious and nutritious meals while minimizing the risk of spoilage or disappointment. Whether you're selecting beef, chicken, seafood, lamb, minced meat, or pork, these guidelines empower you to make informed choices that enhance your culinary experiences and overall satisfaction with grocery shopping.

# Chapter 25. Sample Products Before Buying

When encountering a new food product in a grocery store, it's essential to approach it with a strategy that balances curiosity with caution. The right way to do it is by trying them with an open mind, allowing yourself to discover flavors and textures that may become new favorites. Discovering diverse culinary cultures through new food products can be an enriching experience. Whether it's a new ingredient, flavor profile, or cooking technique, embracing variety broadens your culinary horizons.

Just as judging a book by its cover can be misleading, assuming a new food will suit your tastes based on its packaging alone can lead to disappointment. To mitigate this, it's advisable to begin with small purchases—a single pack or a sample size, if available. This approach allows you to try the product without committing to a larger quantity, minimizing financial risk and potential food waste if it turns out not to be to your liking.

Sampling is another effective way to explore new foods. Many grocery stores offer promotional samples or tasting stations where you can try before you buy. Taking advantage of these opportunities provides a firsthand experience of the product's flavor, texture, and overall appeal. It's a practical step towards ensuring that the food aligns with your palate and culinary expectations before making a purchase decision.

Before purchasing, take a moment to read the labels and product descriptions. This information provides insights into ingredients, nutritional content, and potential allergens, helping you make informed choices. Understanding what the product offers and how it fits into your dietary preferences or restrictions can guide your decision-making process effectively.

Once you've sampled a new food product and confirmed your enjoyment of it, consider purchasing larger quantities for regular use at home. Buying in bulk for items you know you like can be cost-effective and convenient, ensuring you have your favorite foods on hand for meals and snacks.

It's important to acknowledge that not every new food product will suit your tastes. Accepting this as part of your culinary exploration enables you to learn from each experience. If a product doesn't meet your expectations, consider it a learning opportunity rather than a setback. Use these experiences to refine your preferences and make more informed choices in the future.

When exploring new products in a grocery store, it's not just limited to food items that benefit from sampling before buying in bulk. Many non-food items, such as household cleaners, personal care products, and even kitchen gadgets, can also be sampled or tested for suitability before making a larger purchase. Similar to food products, starting with smaller sizes or taking advantage of promotional samples allows you to evaluate the quality, effectiveness, and compatibility of these items with your needs and preferences.

Sampling non-food items before committing to a larger purchase can help you assess factors such as fragrance, texture, durability, and ease of use. For instance, testing a new laundry detergent or skincare product can provide insights into its effectiveness and compatibility with your skin or laundry needs. Likewise, trying out a kitchen appliance or tool before purchasing ensures it meets your expectations in terms of functionality and performance.

Seeking out reviews or recommendations from trusted sources can also provide valuable insights. Food blogs, online forums, or recommendations from friends and family who have tried the product can offer perspectives that complement your own assessment. These insights can validate your interest in the product or raise considerations you might not have initially thought about. Understanding the features, benefits, and potential drawbacks of a product helps in making informed decisions that align with your specific requirements.

In conclusion, approaching new food products with a blend of curiosity and caution allows you to navigate the grocery store with confidence. By starting small, sampling when possible, and gathering information before purchasing, you can make informed decisions that enhance your shopping experiences while minimizing the risk of disappointment and unnecessary expenditures.

# Chapter 26. Grocery Shopping with Dietary Restrictions

Grocery shopping with dietary restrictions requires a clear understanding of your specific needs. Whether you're managing allergies, intolerances, or health conditions, or following a specific dietary lifestyle like veganism or low-carb, knowing what foods are safe and suitable is essential. Start by familiarizing yourself with the ingredients to avoid and those that are safe. This knowledge helps you make informed choices and ensures you stay within your dietary guidelines.

Reading food labels becomes crucial when shopping with dietary restrictions. Learn to decipher labels for allergens and hidden ingredients that may not align with your dietary needs. Look for certifications such as gluten-free, kosher, halal, vegetarian, or organic, which can simplify the process of finding suitable products. Online resources and mobile apps can also assist in identifying allergen-free or specialty items, helping you navigate the aisles more efficiently.

Finding suitable alternatives is key to maintaining a satisfying diet while adhering to restrictions. Explore different brands and products tailored to your dietary requirements. Fresh produce and whole foods often provide natural alternatives that are inherently free from common allergies or dietary triggers. Incorporating variety into your diet ensures you receive adequate nutrition and prevents monotony in meal planning.

Planning meals ahead of time is a practical strategy for ensuring dietary needs are consistently met. Batch cooking and meal prep can save time and effort while guaranteeing you have safe and nutritious options readily available. Include versatile ingredients that align with your restrictions and explore new recipes to keep meals interesting and enjoyable.

Utilizing support from healthcare professionals, dietitians, or nutritionists can provide personalized guidance tailored to your specific dietary needs. These experts can offer advice on managing allergies, optimizing nutritional intake, and navigating social situations or dining out while adhering to restrictions. Online communities and forums also provide valuable insights, recipes, and moral support from others facing similar challenges.

Staying informed about changes in food labeling regulations and advancements in dietary science is essential. This knowledge helps you make informed decisions while adapting to new products or practices that align with your dietary restrictions. Budgeting wisely is another aspect to consider when shopping with dietary restrictions. Look for cost-effective options, compare prices, and take advantage of sales or discounts on specialty items to manage expenses while maintaining dietary integrity.

So be prepared for emergencies related to food allergies or intolerances. Carry necessary medications and inform those around you about your dietary needs to ensure prompt and appropriate assistance if accidental exposure occurs. By integrating these strategies into your grocery shopping routine, you can shop confidently, enjoy a varied diet, and effectively manage your dietary restrictions for optimal health and well-being.

# Chapter 27. Positive Grocery Shopping Etiquette

One of the helpful tips for clever grocery shopping is the way you interact with store staff and fellow shoppers, which plays a crucial role in shaping your overall experience. Adopting a courteous and friendly demeanor can significantly enhance various aspects of your grocery trip.

Firstly, maintaining a polite attitude contributes to a pleasant atmosphere within the store. This positivity not only benefits your own shopping experience but also creates a more enjoyable environment for others. It sets a tone of respect and consideration, fostering a space where everyone can navigate the aisles with ease and comfort. Moreover, being courteous to store staff can lead to improved customer service. When you approach interactions with politeness and friendliness, employees are more likely to respond positively. This may result in better assistance, quicker resolutions to inquiries, and even insider tips on promotions or product recommendations tailored to your preferences.

Building positive relationships with store staff can also enhance your overall shopping efficiency. Employees who recognize and appreciate your respectful demeanor may go out of their way to assist you promptly and efficiently. This can save time and effort during your grocery trip, allowing you to focus more on selecting items and less on potential obstacles or delays. Furthermore, extending courtesy to fellow shoppers contributes to a smoother shopping experience for everyone. Practicing patience, allowing others space to browse, and avoiding actions that could disrupt the flow of traffic in the aisles are all gestures that promote a harmonious shopping environment. By respecting others' needs and shopping styles, you contribute to a more efficient and enjoyable experience for all customers.

Beyond practical benefits, being friendly and courteous during grocery shopping reflects positively on your personal reputation. It demonstrates a level of consideration and community spirit, showing that you value respectful interactions with others. This can lead to positive social interactions and a sense of camaraderie among shoppers, fostering a supportive community atmosphere within the store.

While the act of being courteous and friendly may not directly impact the cost of your groceries, it greatly enhances the overall shopping experience. By creating a positive atmosphere, improving customer service interactions, promoting efficient shopping practices, and fostering community connections, courteous behavior contributes significantly to a successful and enjoyable grocery trip. Making these principles part of your shopping strategy can enrich your overall experience and contribute to a more pleasant environment for everyone involved.

# Chapter 28. Gradual Shopping for Special Occasions

Preparing for special occasions like Christmas, birthdays, or anniversaries requires thoughtful planning to manage time and expenses effectively. By spreading out your shopping over time, you can reduce stress and ensure everything is in place for a memorable celebration.

Start by creating a detailed list of items needed for the occasion. Include gifts, decorations, and ingredients for special meals to prioritize purchases and plan accordingly. This approach helps ensure you cover all essential aspects without overspending or forgetting important details. Organizing your shopping list into categories—such as gifts, groceries, and decorations—provides structure, helping you stay organized and focused.

Take advantage of seasonal sales and promotions throughout the year to purchase gifts and decorations at discounted prices. Planning ahead enables you to capitalize on savings opportunities while still securing high-quality items that fit your budget and preferences. By strategizing your purchases over time, you avoid the last-minute rush and the pressure of inflated prices during peak shopping seasons.

Utilize online shopping options to streamline your shopping experience. Maintain wish lists to track gift ideas and compare prices from various retailers. Many online platforms offer convenient delivery services, allowing you to shop from the comfort of your home and avoid crowded stores. This method not only saves time but also reduces the stress associated with physical shopping trips.

Consider incorporating do-it-yourself (DIY) projects for decorations or personalized gifts to add a special touch to your celebrations while saving money. Engaging in creative activities provides opportunities for meaningful involvement with family and friends, enhancing the overall experience and creating lasting memories.

Remaining flexible in your plans and budget is essential to accommodating unexpected expenses or changes in circumstances. By planning gradually and staying adaptable, you can enjoy special occasions with confidence and happiness. This approach ensures that every detail contributes to a memorable and stress-free celebration, allowing you to focus on enjoying time with loved ones.

For instance, if you're planning for Christmas, starting early allows you to purchase decorations and gifts gradually, spreading out the financial burden and avoiding last-minute stress. You can also take advantage of off-season sales to stock up on items like wrapping paper and ornaments, ensuring you're prepared well in advance.

Birthdays and anniversaries benefit similarly from gradual planning. By creating a timeline for purchasing gifts and planning meals, you can manage expenses more effectively and tailor your celebrations to fit your budget. This method also gives you the flexibility to adjust plans as needed, ensuring a memorable and enjoyable occasion for everyone involved.

Gradual shopping for special occasions is a wise choice that enhances your ability to plan effectively, manage expenses wisely, and create memorable celebrations. By spreading out your shopping tasks, utilizing sales and online shopping options, and incorporating DIY projects, you can reduce stress, save money, and ensure that every detail contributes to a meaningful and enjoyable event.

# Chapter 29. Communication with Store Staff

One of the most valuable resources available to shoppers in any grocery store is the knowledgeable staff who work there. Whether you're looking for specific product information, seeking recommendations, or simply needing assistance navigating the aisles, engaging with store staff can greatly enhance your shopping experience.

When you enter a grocery store with a particular product in mind but are unsure about its location or specifics, approaching a staff member can provide immediate clarity. They can guide you to the correct aisle or section where the product is stocked, saving you time and effort wandering around the store. Their familiarity with the store layout and inventory ensures that you can locate items efficiently, especially during busy shopping periods.

Beyond locating products, store staff are valuable sources of information about the products themselves. Whether you're interested in understanding ingredients, nutritional content, allergens, or production methods, they can provide detailed insights to help you make informed decisions. This is particularly important if you have dietary restrictions, allergies, or specific preferences regarding food quality or sourcing.

Moreover, store staff often have firsthand knowledge of new or seasonal products that may not yet be widely advertised. They can inform you about special promotions, discounts, or upcoming sales that could save you money on your purchases. By staying informed through their recommendations, you can take advantage of opportunities to try new products or stock up on essentials at reduced prices.

In addition to product knowledge, store staff can offer personalized recommendations based on your preferences and needs. Whether you're looking for a wine pairing for a special dinner, a healthy snack option, or a gift idea, their expertise allows them to suggest suitable products that meet your criteria. This personalized service adds value to your shopping experience by tailoring recommendations to your specific requirements.

Furthermore, engaging with store staff fosters a sense of community and customer care. Building rapport with employees creates a welcoming environment where you feel valued as a shopper. They can address any concerns or questions you may have, ensuring that you leave the store satisfied with your purchases and overall experience.

Asking for product information and recommendations from store staff not only enhances the efficiency of your shopping trip but also enriches your understanding of the products available. Their expertise enables you to make informed choices that align with your preferences and dietary needs. By leveraging their knowledge and insights, you can maximize the benefits of your grocery shopping experience and enjoy greater satisfaction with your purchases.

# Chapter 30. Shopping with Organization

Efficiently organizing your grocery shopping can significantly enhance your overall experience and streamline the process from start to finish. One practical approach is to begin by selecting non-food items first. This method allows you to prioritize items such as household essentials, cleaning supplies, or personal care products that are not perishable. By tackling these purchases initially, you can proceed to shop for fresh and frozen produce without concerns about them thawing or losing quality during an extended shopping trip.

Dividing your shopping list into sections based on categories is another effective strategy. Organize your list to include separate sections for produce, pantry staples, dairy products, meats, and non-food items. This structured approach helps you shop in the store more efficiently, reducing the likelihood of overlooking essential items and minimizing the need to backtrack or make multiple rounds through the aisles.

Separating food and non-food items during your shopping trip also simplifies the packing process. As you progress through your list, place non-food items neatly in your shopping bags or cart. This organization ensures that these items are readily accessible during checkout and makes it easier to load them into your vehicle afterward. Upon arriving home, this separation saves time and effort by allowing you to promptly place food items in their designated spots in the kitchen and non-food items in their appropriate storage areas throughout your home.

Furthermore, organizing your shopping in this manner contributes to a more efficient checkout process. Grouping items logically on the conveyor belt at the register facilitates quicker scanning and packing, which expedites your departure from the store. This not only saves time but also minimizes potential stress associated with delays or disorganization at the checkout counter.

By adopting these detailed strategies for organizing your grocery trips, you can optimize efficiency, reduce stress, and ensure that your purchases are handled and stored appropriately upon returning home. Planning your shopping journey section by section according to your list not only enhances your overall shopping experience but also promotes a sense of satisfaction and accomplishment as you navigate through the store with purpose and clarity.

# Chapter 31. Using Thermal Bags and Cooler Boxes

When shopping for groceries, especially during the hot summer months when temperatures outside soar, it's crucial to take proactive steps to prevent food from spoiling or thawing prematurely. One effective strategy is to utilize thermal bags and cooler boxes during your shopping trips. These insulated containers help maintain the temperature of perishable items such as fresh produce, dairy products, meats, and frozen goods, ensuring they remain at safe temperatures until you reach home.

Thermal bags and cooler boxes act as a protective barrier against external heat, preserving the freshness and quality of your groceries during transportation. By keeping perishable items cool, you mitigate the risk of food spoilage and the associated financial loss that comes with having to discard spoiled food. This proactive measure also alleviates the stress and inconvenience of rushing home to refrigerate or freeze items quickly.

During hot weather, the interior temperature of a car can rise rapidly, potentially causing perishable items to spoil or thaw if left unprotected. Thermal bags and cooler boxes are a practical solution because they provide an insulated environment that helps regulate the temperature of your groceries. This ensures that sensitive items like dairy, meats, and frozen goods maintain their integrity and safety until you are ready to store them properly at home.

Moreover, incorporating thermal bags and cooler boxes into your shopping routine promotes sustainability by reducing food waste. By preserving the freshness of perishable items, you minimize the need to discard spoiled food, which in turn contributes to environmental conservation efforts.

Using thermal bags and cooler boxes for grocery shopping, particularly in hot weather, is a proactive measure that safeguards your purchases from premature spoilage or thawing. By maintaining optimal temperatures during transit, you protect your investment in groceries, reduce food waste, and ensure a more pleasant and stress-free shopping experience overall.

# Chapter 32. Late-Night Grocery Discounts

Shopping smart is not just about finding the right deals but also knowing when and where to shop to maximize your savings. One strategy that many savvy shoppers swear by is hitting the grocery store during the late evening hours. This timing can often lead to discounts on various items, ranging from fresh produce like fruits and vegetables to bakery items such as bread and dairy products.

Picture this: it's nearing closing time at your local grocery store. The bustling aisles from earlier in the day have quieted down, and the store is keen to sell off perishable items before they have to be discarded. This is where you, the smart shopper, can benefit.

One of the most significant potential savings can be found in the produce section. Fruits and vegetables that are ripe but haven't been sold throughout the day may be marked down to prevent spoilage. You might find deals on items like perfectly ripe avocados, tomatoes, or berries that are just past their peak freshness but still perfectly good for consumption. These discounts can make a significant difference if you enjoy fresh produce but find it expensive at regular prices.

Similarly, bakery items like bread and pastries often see price reductions later in the day. Many bakeries and grocery store bakery departments bake fresh items daily and prefer to sell them fresh. By the end of the day, what hasn't sold may be offered at a discount. This is a great opportunity to snag artisan loaves, baguettes, or even specialty pastries that might otherwise be out of your budget.

Dairy products, too, can be subject to markdowns in the evening. Items like yogurt nearing their expiration dates or cheeses that need to be sold quickly might be offered at reduced prices. These products are usually perfectly safe to consume for several days beyond the sell-by date, making them a smart buy if you plan to use them promptly.

Apart from specific categories, shopping late can also offer other advantages. The overall atmosphere tends to be quieter and more relaxed, allowing you to browse at your own pace without the rush of crowds. This can lead to a more enjoyable shopping experience and give you the chance to carefully inspect items for quality without feeling pressured.

Moreover, late-night shopping can sometimes coincide with store promotions or clearance events. Some stores schedule clearance markdowns in the evenings to prepare for new inventory, meaning you might stumble upon deeply discounted items across various departments. Keeping an eye out for these promotions can further enhance your savings.

Of course, there are considerations to keep in mind when adopting this shopping strategy. While many grocery stores do reduce prices towards closing time, not all items may be marked down, and the extent of discounts can vary. It's also essential to be mindful of freshness and quality. While discounted items are generally safe and edible, always check for signs of spoilage or damage before making a purchase.

Timing your grocery shopping late in the evening can also require some adjustments to your schedule. If you're used to shopping during the day, switching to evening hours might take some getting used to. However, if saving money is a priority for you, the potential benefits of late-night shopping can outweigh the inconvenience.

Another tip for maximizing your savings is to keep an eye out for clearance or manager's specials throughout the store. These are often located in designated sections and can include everything from canned goods to household items. By taking the time to explore these areas, you may discover unexpected bargains that can help stretch your grocery budget further.

Shopping during late-night hours at grocery stores can indeed offer savings on a variety of items, including fresh produce, bakery goods, dairy products, and more. By taking advantage of reduced prices on items nearing their sell-by dates or end-of-day discounts, you can enjoy quality products at a fraction of their original cost. Combine this strategy with careful planning and awareness of store promotions to make the most of your grocery shopping experience while saving money effectively.

# Chapter 33. Avoid Excess Buying of Discounted Items

Shopping for discounted items can be a double-edged sword. On one hand, it's an opportunity to save money and possibly afford items that might otherwise be out of budget. On the other hand, it's easy to fall into the trap of buying things simply because they're on sale, rather than because they are truly needed or beneficial. It's important to understand the pitfalls of excess buying during sales and offer strategies for making more intentional and economical shopping decisions.

Discounts have a powerful allure. Whether it's a clearance rack filled with heavily marked-down clothing or a grocery store aisle stacked with items nearing their expiration dates, the promise of savings can lead even the most budget-conscious shopper astray. Retailers strategically use discounts to attract customers, clear out excess inventory, and stimulate sales during slower periods. While this benefits both businesses and consumers in many ways, it's essential for shoppers to approach discounted shopping with a discerning eye.

Psychologically, discounts trigger a sense of urgency and excitement in consumers. The fear of missing out on a good deal (FOMO) can prompt impulse purchases, even when there is no immediate need for the item. Retailers capitalize on this by creating a sense of scarcity or limited-time offers, pushing consumers to buy now rather than later. Moreover, the perceived value of getting something at a lower price often overrides rational considerations about whether the item is necessary or adds genuine value to one's life.

One of the most significant pitfalls of excessive shopping during sales is the accumulation of unnecessary items. Buying things simply because they are on sale can lead to clutter in our homes and unnecessary strain on our finances. It's not uncommon for discounted purchases to end up forgotten in the back of a closet or pantry, never to be used or appreciated. This phenomenon, known as "sale goggles," refers to the distorted perception that everything on sale must be a good buy, regardless of its actual utility or value.

Contrary to popular belief, excessive shopping during sales can actually lead to wasting money rather than saving it. The initial thrill of scoring a bargain can quickly fade when the reality sets in that the purchased items were unnecessary or redundant. In essence, spending money on things we don't need, even if they are discounted, is still spending money unnecessarily. This undermines the very purpose of saving through discounts.

To avoid falling into the trap of excess buying during sales, it's important to develop strategies that promote mindful shopping and financial responsibility. Before heading to a store or browsing online, make a list of items you genuinely need or have been planning to purchase. This helps you focus your attention and resist the temptation of impulse buys.

Determine how much you can afford to spend on discounted items without compromising your overall financial goals. Stick to this budget strictly to prevent overspending. Before making a purchase, ask yourself if the item is something you truly need or if it's more of a want driven by the allure of the discount. Be honest with yourself about whether the purchase will genuinely improve your life or if it's just a fleeting desire.

Assess the long-term value of the discounted item. Will it serve a practical purpose over time, or will its appeal be short-lived? Investing in quality items that fulfill genuine needs is often more cost-effective in the long run than buying cheaply made goods just because they're on sale. Be mindful of your emotions when shopping. Take a moment to pause and reflect on whether the urge to buy is driven by genuine necessity or by emotional factors such as stress, boredom, or the desire for instant gratification.

If you're uncertain about a purchase, allow yourself a period of time to reconsider. Delaying the decision allows you to reconsider whether the item is truly worth purchasing, even at a discounted price. Practice intentional shopping by focusing on items that align with your values and priorities. This approach not only helps prevent impulse buys but also ensures that your purchases contribute positively to your life.

While discounted items can offer significant savings, it's crucial to approach sales with a balanced perspective. Avoiding excess buying during sales involves understanding the psychology of discounts, recognizing the difference between saving money and wasting it, and developing strategies for making intentional shopping decisions. By doing so, you can harness the benefits of discounts without falling prey to unnecessary spending or clutter, ultimately achieving a more sustainable and financially sound shopping habit.

# Chapter 34. Efficient Meal Planning

Meal planning is a cornerstone of efficient household management, offering numerous benefits beyond just saving time and money. It involves strategic organization and foresight to optimize grocery purchases while minimizing food waste. By carefully planning meals ahead of time, individuals and families can streamline their shopping trips, ensure they have all necessary ingredients on hand, and reduce the likelihood of impulse purchases that can lead to overspending.

One of the primary advantages of meal planning is its ability to foster healthier eating habits. When meals are planned in advance, there's a greater opportunity to balance nutrition and variety. This can help individuals avoid the temptation of quick, less nutritious options that may be more convenient but less beneficial in the long run. By consciously choosing recipes that incorporate a variety of fruits, vegetables, lean proteins, and whole grains, meal planners can create well-rounded menus that support overall health and well-being.

Efficiency in meal planning also extends to financial savings. By outlining meals for the week or month, individuals can create a shopping list that aligns with their budget and prevents unnecessary purchases. This proactive approach reduces the likelihood of buying items that may only be used once or forgotten in the pantry, ultimately saving money by minimizing food waste.

Moreover, meal planning contributes to environmental sustainability by reducing food waste. When meals are thoughtfully planned, individuals are less likely to buy excess food that may spoil before it can be consumed. This not only conserves natural resources used in food production but also decreases the amount of food sent to landfills, where it contributes to methane emissions and environmental degradation.

Effective meal planning starts with setting aside dedicated time to plan meals and create a shopping list. Many people find it helpful to designate a specific day each week for meal planning, such as Sunday afternoon or evening. During this time, they review recipes, check their pantry and refrigerator for existing ingredients, and identify any additional items needed for upcoming meals. This structured approach ensures that nothing is overlooked and that meals can be prepared efficiently throughout the week.

Variety is another key aspect of successful meal planning. While consistency can simplify shopping and preparation, incorporating diverse flavors and cuisines keeps meals interesting and enjoyable. Experimenting with new recipes and ingredients not only expands culinary horizons but also encourages healthier eating habits by introducing a wider range of nutrients and flavors into daily meals.

Flexibility is also important in meal planning. Life is unpredictable, and schedules can change unexpectedly. Having a flexible meal plan allows for adjustments as needed, such as swapping planned meals between days or using ingredients in different recipes to accommodate last-minute changes. This adaptability helps prevent food waste and ensures that meals remain enjoyable and satisfying despite unforeseen circumstances.

Another strategy for efficient meal planning is batch cooking and meal preparation. Batch cooking involves preparing larger quantities of food at once, which can then be portioned and stored for future meals. This approach not only saves time during busy weekdays but also reduces the need for frequent cooking and cleanup. Meal prepping takes batch cooking a step further by portioning meals into individual servings that are ready to heat and eat, making it ideal for individuals with hectic schedules or limited time for cooking.

Incorporating seasonal produce into meal planning can also enhance both flavor and affordability. Seasonal fruits and vegetables are often more abundant and less expensive when they are in peak season. By planning meals around seasonal ingredients, individuals can take advantage of fresh, flavorful produce while supporting local farmers and reducing their carbon footprint.

Technology can be a valuable tool in modern meal planning. Many apps and websites offer meal planning templates, recipe databases, and automated shopping lists that streamline the planning process. These tools allow users to quickly browse recipes, adjust serving sizes, and generate shopping lists based on selected meals. Some apps even provide nutritional information and dietary recommendations to help users make informed choices about their meals.

Moreover, involving family members in the meal planning process can promote collaboration and encourage healthier eating habits among children and adults alike. By soliciting input from family members about their favorite meals or dietary preferences, planners can create menus that are both nutritious and appealing to everyone at the table. This collaborative approach fosters a sense of shared responsibility for meal preparation and encourages family members to take an active role in their own health and well-being.

Meal planning is indeed a valuable tool for optimizing grocery purchases, minimizing food waste, and promoting healthier eating habits. By dedicating time to plan meals, create shopping lists, and incorporate variety and seasonal ingredients, individuals can streamline their meal preparation process, save money, and reduce their environmental impact. Whether using traditional methods or leveraging technology, effective meal planning empowers individuals to make informed choices about their food consumption while enjoying flavorful, nutritious meals that support overall health and well-being.

# Chapter 35. DIY Kitchen Staples for Savings and Flavor

In the realm of grocery shopping savvy, one of the most impactful strategies is crafting your own kitchen staples at home. This approach not only allows for significant savings but also offers the opportunity to tailor flavors and ingredients to suit personal preferences. From bread and sauces to snacks and beyond, creating these essentials from scratch can transform your culinary experience while optimizing your budget.

Let's begin with bread, a staple found in most households. Homemade bread not only boasts superior flavor and texture compared to store-bought varieties but also allows you to control the ingredients used. Basic bread recipes typically require flour, water, yeast, and salt—simple components that, when combined and baked at home, result in a delicious loaf that far surpasses many commercial options. Additionally, making bread at home is cost-effective, especially when considering the price of artisanal or specialty breads at supermarkets.

Sauces and condiments are another area where DIY can make a significant impact. Many store-bought sauces and condiments contain additives, preservatives, and high levels of sodium or sugar. By making them at home, you can adjust the flavors to your liking and eliminate unwanted ingredients. For instance, a homemade marinara sauce can be crafted from fresh tomatoes, garlic, herbs, and olive oil, ensuring a healthier and more flavorful alternative to jarred varieties. Similarly, homemade salad dressings, like vinaigrettes or creamy dressings, offer endless possibilities for customization while avoiding artificial additives.

Snacks are often a source of convenience, but they can also be a drain on the grocery budget. Making snacks at home allows you to control portion sizes, nutritional content, and ingredients. For example, granola bars, energy bites, and popcorn can all be prepared with wholesome ingredients like oats, nuts, seeds, and natural sweeteners such as honey or maple syrup. These homemade snacks not only save money compared to pre-packaged alternatives but also provide a healthier option for snacking throughout the day.

Furthermore, creating DIY kitchen staples aligns with broader trends toward sustainability and reducing packaging waste. By making items like bread, sauces, and snacks at home, you can reduce your reliance on single-use packaging and minimize your environmental footprint. This eco-friendly approach contributes to a more sustainable lifestyle while promoting mindful consumption habits.

Beyond financial and environmental benefits, DIY kitchen staples offer a rewarding culinary experience. Experimenting with different recipes and flavors allows for creativity in the kitchen and the satisfaction of mastering traditional techniques. Baking bread, for instance, can become a therapeutic ritual that connects you to food preparation on a deeper level, fostering a sense of accomplishment with each successful loaf.

Practical tips can help streamline the process of making DIY kitchen staples. Planning ahead and batching recipes can save time and effort. For example, making a double batch of bread dough and freezing half for later baking ensures a steady supply of fresh bread without daily preparation. Similarly, preparing large batches of sauces or snacks and storing them in portioned containers or freezer bags allows for convenient access to homemade options throughout the week.

Moreover, investing in basic kitchen tools and equipment can enhance your ability to create DIY staples efficiently. A good-quality bread pan, blender or food processor for sauces, and storage containers for snacks are essential items that can make the homemade process easier and more enjoyable. These tools not only facilitate preparation but also contribute to long-term savings by reducing reliance on store-bought equivalents.

For those new to DIY cooking, starting with simple recipes and gradually expanding your repertoire can build confidence and skill over time. Online resources, such as recipe websites, cooking blogs, and video tutorials, offer a wealth of inspiration and guidance for beginners. Learning fundamental techniques, such as bread kneading or sauce simmering, lays the groundwork for more complex culinary endeavors and allows for greater experimentation with flavors and ingredients.

Using DIY kitchen staples is a practical and rewarding approach to clever grocery shopping. By creating bread, sauces, snacks, and other essentials at home, individuals can save money, customize flavors to personal preferences, and reduce their environmental impact. This homemade approach aligns with trends toward healthier eating, sustainability, and culinary creativity, making it a valuable addition to any savvy shopper's repertoire. Whether you're drawn to the aroma of freshly baked bread or the satisfaction of crafting a perfect marinara sauce, exploring DIY kitchen staples offers a pathway to culinary satisfaction and financial efficiency alike.

# Chapter 36. Healthy Eating on a Budget

Maintaining a nutritious diet while staying within your budget requires strategic planning and smart shopping habits. By prioritizing wholesome ingredients and efficient meal preparation, you can enjoy healthy eating without straining your finances. Here's a comprehensive guide to eating well on a budget, complete with practical tips and a variety of delicious recipes to inspire your culinary journey.

To begin with, effective meal planning is crucial. By mapping out your meals for the week ahead, you can create a targeted shopping list based on what you need. This approach minimizes impulse purchases and ensures you have all the ingredients on hand for nutritious meals throughout the week.

Buying staple items such as rice, beans, oats, and whole grains in bulk is another savvy strategy. These items are not only cost-effective but also versatile, forming the foundation for many meals. Opting for seasonal fruits and vegetables is also recommended. In-season produce tends to be cheaper and fresher than out-of-season options, allowing you to stretch your grocery budget further.

Frozen and canned fruits and vegetables are nutritious alternatives to fresh produce, offering a longer shelf life and often costing less. Incorporating these items into your meal planning can help you maintain a balanced diet without exceeding your budget. Cooking at home is generally more economical than dining out or purchasing pre-made meals. Learning basic cooking skills empowers you to prepare affordable and nutritious meals tailored to your preferences.

Comparing prices across different brands and stores enables you to capitalize on sales, discounts, and coupons. This practice ensures you're getting the best deals on your grocery purchases. Additionally, limiting purchases of processed foods and snacks can contribute to both financial savings and improved nutrition. Whole ingredients are typically more affordable and offer greater nutritional value compared to processed alternatives.

For those with the space and inclination, growing herbs, vegetables, or fruits at home can further reduce grocery expenses while providing access to fresh produce. This approach not only saves money but also fosters a connection to the food you eat. Meal prep is another effective strategy for budget-friendly eating. By preparing meals in advance and storing them in portioned containers, you save time during busy weekdays and minimize the temptation to dine out.

Affordable sources of protein, such as beans, lentils, eggs, canned fish, and tofu, are valuable additions to your diet. These options are not only budget-friendly but also rich in essential nutrients. Incorporating them into your meals ensures balanced nutrition without compromising your financial goals.

Now, let's explore some budget-friendly recipes to inspire your meal planning:

For breakfast, try Banana Oat Pancakes made with rolled oats, ripe bananas, eggs, baking powder, and cinnamon. Blend oats into flour, mix with mashed bananas and other ingredients, and cook until golden brown for a hearty and nutritious start to your day.

For lunch, consider chickpea salad wraps using canned chickpeas, Greek yogurt, celery, red onion, lettuce leaves, and whole wheat wraps. Mix mashed chickpeas with yogurt and vegetables, spoon onto lettuce leaves, and wrap for a satisfying and portable meal.

Dinner options include One-Pan Chicken and Vegetables, featuring chicken breasts, mixed vegetables, olive oil, herbs, salt, and pepper. Season and bake everything on a single sheet pan for easy cleanup and a delicious meal.

For snacks, homemade hummus with veggies is a nutritious choice. Blend chickpeas, tahini, lemon juice, garlic, and olive oil until smooth, and serve with sliced vegetables for dipping.

Greek Yogurt Parfait is another great snack or dessert option, layered with yogurt, granola, mixed berries, and honey for a sweet and satisfying treat.

By incorporating these tips and recipes into your routine, you can enjoy healthy eating on a budget that supports both your well-being and your financial goals. Experiment with flavors and ingredients to discover delicious and affordable meals that nourish your body and mind. With a focus on smart shopping and nutritious choices, eating well doesn't have to be expensive or complicated—it can be a rewarding and enjoyable part of your everyday life.

# Chapter 37. Buying at Farmers Markets

Shopping at farmer's markets offers a unique experience that goes beyond traditional grocery shopping. It's an opportunity to connect directly with local farmers and artisans, support the community, and access fresh, seasonal produce. Here's a comprehensive guide to help you navigate farmer's markets and make the most of your shopping experience.

When you visit a farmer's market, arrive early for the best selection. Farmers often bring limited quantities of specialty items, so getting there early ensures you have a wide variety to choose from. It's also a great way to interact with farmers and producers when they are less busy and can provide insights into their products.

One of the primary advantages of shopping at farmer's markets is access to seasonal produce. Unlike supermarkets that offer fruits and vegetables year-round, farmer's markets feature items that are freshly harvested and in season. Seasonal produce not only tastes better but is often more affordable due to its abundance during peak harvest times.

To make the most of seasonal produce, familiarize yourself with what grows locally and when it's in season. Spring might bring vibrant greens like asparagus and spinach, while summer showcases juicy tomatoes and sweet berries. Fall offers an abundance of squash, pumpkins, and apples, while winter features hearty root vegetables like carrots and potatoes.

Before you go, consider bringing cash in small denominations. While some farmer's markets accept cards or mobile payments, cash is often preferred and can help you make quicker transactions. Additionally, bring reusable bags or baskets to carry your purchases, as they are environmentally friendly and easier to manage than plastic bags.

When you arrive at the market, take a leisurely stroll to survey what each vendor offers before making purchases. This enables you to make comparisons between prices and quality, ensuring that you obtain optimal value for your money. Keep an eye out for "seconds" or slightly imperfect produce, which vendors often sell at a discount but are still perfectly good for cooking or preserving.

Engaging with farmers and vendors is a key aspect of the farmer's market experience. Don't hesitate to ask questions about how products are grown or produced. Many vendors are proud to share their farming practices, whether they use organic methods, practice sustainable agriculture, or have unique varieties of produce.

Supporting local growers is another significant benefit of shopping at farmer's markets. By purchasing directly from farmers, you contribute to the local economy and help sustain small-scale agriculture. This direct relationship fosters community connections and promotes food security by reducing dependence on long-distance food transportation.

Beyond fresh produce, farmer's markets often feature a diverse array of artisanal products, such as handmade crafts, baked goods, preserves, cheeses, and meats. These items are typically made with care and attention to quality, making them unique additions to your shopping list and perfect for supporting local artisans.

To optimize your shopping experience, consider planning meals around what's available at the market. Flexibility is key, as the selection may vary from week to week based on seasonal availability and vendor offerings. Experimenting with new recipes based on what you find can inspire creativity in the kitchen and introduce you to new flavors and ingredients.

If you're unsure how to prepare a particular vegetable or fruit, don't hesitate to ask vendors for recipe ideas or cooking tips. They are often passionate about their products and eager to share their knowledge. You might discover new ways to incorporate seasonal produce into your meals, enhancing both taste and nutrition.

When you're ready to make a purchase, be mindful of quantities. Buying in bulk at farmer's markets can sometimes lead to waste if you're unable to consume or preserve perishable items before they spoil. Consider your household's needs and storage capabilities when deciding how much to buy.

After shopping, take a moment to reflect on your experience and the connections you've made with local farmers and vendors. Farmer's markets offer more than just food—they provide a sense of community, sustainability, and appreciation for locally sourced goods.

Shopping at farmer's markets is indeed a rewarding experience that supports local agriculture, promotes seasonal eating, and connects you with fresh, high-quality produce. By following these tips and embracing the diversity of offerings, you can navigate farmer's markets confidently and enjoy the benefits of wholesome, locally sourced food.

# Chapter 38. Smart Grocery Shopping Abroad

When traveling abroad, whether for holidays or other reasons, taking advantage of your trip to save money on grocery shopping can be a smart strategy. Here's how you can make the most of your trip by stocking up on goodies and food items that might be cheaper or more unique compared to what you find at home.

Before you travel, research local markets, supermarkets, and specialty stores at your destination. This helps you identify items that are typically more affordable or of higher quality compared to what's available in your hometown or country. Make a list of items you want to purchase, such as nuts, spices, honey, herbs, chocolates, candies, and other non-perishable goods.

Check your airline's baggage allowance policy to determine how much luggage you can bring without incurring extra fees. If your allowance permits, consider packing an empty suitcase or leaving extra space in your luggage specifically for items you plan to bring back home. Be mindful of weight restrictions to avoid exceeding limits and incurring additional charges.

During your trip, visit local markets and farmers' markets, where you can find fresh produce, spices, and handmade goods at competitive prices. Vendors often sell items that reflect the region's culinary specialties and cultural heritage. Compare prices between different stores and markets to ensure you're getting the best deals. Take note of any special offers, discounts, or bulk purchase options that can maximize your savings.

Focus on purchasing non-perishable items that travel well and have a longer shelf life. This includes spices, dried herbs, canned goods, chocolates, and packaged snacks that you can enjoy or share with friends and family back home. Explore local delicacies and unique food products that are not readily available in your hometown. This could include artisanal cheeses, cured meats, specialty pastries, or regional wines and spirits.

When packing food items in your luggage, ensure they are securely wrapped and sealed to prevent spills or damage during transit. Use resealable bags, containers, or packing materials like bubble wrap to protect fragile items. Be aware of any customs regulations regarding the importation of food products into your home country to avoid any issues upon your return.

Set a budget for your shopping expenses and exchange currencies before you travel to take advantage of favorable exchange rates. Use credit cards or local currency for larger purchases, and keep small bills or coins handy for transactions at markets or smaller shops. Respect local customs and traditions when shopping and interacting with vendors. Ask for recommendations or advice from locals regarding the best places to shop for groceries and food items.

Engaging with vendors can also provide insight into the cultural significance of certain products and how they are used in local cuisine. Take advantage of duty-free shopping opportunities at airports or border crossings, where you can purchase goods at tax-free or reduced tax rates. Look for promotions or sales events that coincide with your travel dates to further stretch your budget.

Shopping for groceries and food items while abroad can be a rewarding experience that allows you to discover new flavors, save money on familiar items, and bring a taste of your travels back home. By planning ahead, leveraging your baggage allowance, and exploring local markets, you can enjoy the benefits of international shopping while creating lasting memories of your journey.

# Chapter 39. Specialty and Ethnic Grocery Shopping

Specialty and ethnic grocery stores offer a treasure trove of unique ingredients and savings opportunities for adventurous shoppers. These stores specialize in carrying products from specific regions or cultures, providing an authentic taste of cuisines from around the world right in your neighborhood.

One of the main draws of specialty and ethnic grocery stores is the variety of food items available. You can find fresh produce, spices, herbs, sauces, condiments, grains, and meats that are not typically found in mainstream supermarkets. These ingredients are often integral to traditional dishes and recipes from different countries and cultures, allowing you to experiment with new flavors and expand your culinary repertoire.

Shopping at these stores can also be a practical way to save money. Many specialty and ethnic groceries offer competitive prices on staples and specialty items, especially those that are imported or harder to find elsewhere. Buying spices, grains, or specialty sauces in bulk can be significantly cheaper than purchasing smaller quantities from regular supermarkets.

Beyond food, specialty and ethnic grocery stores often stock a wide range of household goods, kitchenware, and unique products from the respective regions. This includes ceramics, utensils, cookbooks, and decorative items that reflect the cultural heritage of the products they sell. Exploring these stores can be an enriching cultural experience, allowing you to learn about different traditions and customs related to food and daily life.

For those passionate about cooking or looking to recreate authentic international dishes at home, these stores are invaluable resources. You can find everything you need to prepare meals from various cuisines, whether it's Japanese sushi ingredients, Indian spices for curry dishes, or Mexican chilies and tortillas. The availability of these ingredients enables you to experiment with different cooking techniques and broaden your culinary skills.

Moreover, shopping at specialty and ethnic grocery stores supports local businesses and communities. Many of these stores are family-owned or operated by individuals who are passionate about sharing their culture through food. By patronizing these establishments, you contribute to the preservation of culinary traditions and help create a vibrant and diverse food landscape in your area.

Exploring specialty and ethnic grocery stores offers more than just a shopping trip—it's an opportunity to discover new and exciting flavors, save money on unique ingredients, and immerse yourself in cultural experiences from around the globe. Whether you're looking for fresh produce, exotic spices, or kitchenware, these stores provide a gateway to culinary adventures that can enhance your cooking skills and enrich your appreciation for global cuisine.

# Chapter 40. Making Organic and Sustainable Choices

Making informed decisions about organic and sustainably sourced products while on a budget requires careful consideration and awareness of various factors. When shopping for organic products, look for certifications such as USDA Organic (United States), EU Organic (European Union), or equivalent labels in your region. These certifications ensure that the product has been grown and processed without synthetic pesticides, herbicides, or genetically modified organisms (GMOs). For sustainable products, certifications like Fair Trade, Rainforest Alliance, or Marine Stewardship Council (MSC) indicate that the item was sourced responsibly, considering environmental, social, and economic impacts.

Focus on prioritizing which products are most important to buy organic or sustainably sourced based on factors like pesticide residues, environmental impact, and personal health considerations. For instance, prioritize organic for items known to have high pesticide residues when conventionally grown, such as berries, spinach, and apples. Choose seasonal and locally sourced produce whenever it's available. These items are often fresher, require less transportation, and support local farmers. Visit farmers' markets or join a community-supported agriculture (CSA) program to access affordable organic or sustainably grown fruits and vegetables directly from local producers.

Look for budget-friendly options such as store brands or generic versions of organic products, which may be more affordable than name brands. Buying in bulk for non-perishable items like grains, beans, or spices can also reduce costs per unit. Consider joining a co-op or subscription service that offers discounts on organic or sustainable products for members. Making meals from scratch using whole ingredients is not only healthier but also more cost-effective than buying pre-packaged or processed foods. Grow your own herbs or vegetables if space allows, or consider preserving seasonal produce to enjoy year-round.

Take the time to educate yourself about sustainable farming practices, fair trade certifications, and the benefits of organic agriculture. Understanding these concepts can empower you to make informed choices and advocate for sustainable practices within your community. Choose brands and companies that prioritize sustainability and ethical practices throughout their supply chains. Research their commitments to environmental stewardship, fair labor practices, and animal welfare to align with your values.

Minimize food waste by planning meals, using leftovers creatively, and storing perishable items properly. This not only saves money but also reduces your environmental footprint by conserving resources used in food production and transportation. Engage with local policymakers and businesses to advocate for increased availability and affordability of organic and sustainable products in your community. Support initiatives that promote sustainable agriculture and reduce the environmental impact of food production.

Making informed decisions about organic and sustainably sourced products on a budget requires a balanced approach that considers health, environmental impact, and affordability. By prioritizing purchases, seeking budget-friendly options, and supporting sustainable practices, you can contribute to a healthier planet while making choices that align with your values and budgetary constraints.

# Chapter 41. Cooking for One or Two

Cooking for one or two individuals offers a unique set of challenges and opportunities compared to preparing meals for larger households. Whether you're living alone, with a partner, or as a couple, effective grocery shopping and meal preparation strategies can help streamline your culinary experience, minimize waste, and ensure you enjoy delicious and satisfying meals on a regular basis.

When you're shopping for a smaller household, thoughtful planning is key to making the most of your shopping trips and ensuring you have the ingredients you need without overbuying. One of the first steps is to create a weekly or bi-weekly meal plan. This plan serves as a roadmap for your grocery list, helping you to stay focused on purchasing items that align with your planned meals and avoiding impulse buys.

Make a list of the meals you intend to prepare for the upcoming week, taking into account breakfasts, lunches, dinners, and any snacks. This approach not only saves time but also reduces the likelihood of purchasing items that may go unused and end up being wasted. Consider incorporating versatile ingredients that can be used in multiple dishes throughout the week, such as chicken breasts that can be grilled for salads or stir-fries.

When it comes to perishable items like fruits, vegetables, and dairy products, consider shopping more frequently throughout the week to ensure freshness. Smaller, more frequent trips to the grocery store or local farmers' markets can help you maintain a steady supply of fresh ingredients while reducing the risk of spoilage.

For pantry staples and non-perishable items, buying in bulk can be a cost-effective strategy. Staples like rice, pasta, beans, and canned goods can be purchased in larger quantities and stored for future use. Be mindful, however, of the shelf life of these items and ensure you have adequate storage space to accommodate bulk purchases.

Efficient meal preparation is essential when cooking for one or two people to save time and effort during the week. One effective strategy is to embrace batch cooking. Prepare larger quantities of meals that can be divided into individual portions and stored in the refrigerator or freezer for later consumption.

Meals that freeze well include soups, stews, casseroles, and sauces. Invest in quality freezer-safe containers or resealable bags to portion and store these meals properly. Label containers with the contents and date to keep track of what you have on hand and ensure food safety.

Leftovers can also be repurposed creatively into new dishes to prevent monotony. For example, leftover roasted chicken can be shredded and used in tacos or sandwiches the next day. Cooked grains like quinoa or rice can be incorporated into salads or stir-fries for quick and nutritious meals.

Plan meals that utilize similar ingredients to minimize waste and ensure everything gets used. For example, if you're making a salad with fresh greens and vegetables, plan to use the remaining ingredients in a stir-fry or soup later in the week. This approach not only reduces food waste but also saves money by maximizing the use of each ingredient.

Experiment with new recipes and cooking techniques to keep meals interesting and enjoyable. Cooking for a smaller household allows for more flexibility and creativity in the kitchen. Use this opportunity to try new cuisines or adapt recipes to suit your taste preferences and dietary needs.

Reducing food waste is a priority when cooking for one or two people. Proper storage of perishable items like fruits, vegetables, and dairy products is crucial to maintaining freshness and extending shelf life. Use airtight containers or resealable bags to store leftovers and ingredients that aren't used immediately.

Plan meals that utilize perishable items before they spoil. For example, if you buy a bunch of spinach for a recipe, plan a second meal later in the week that incorporates the remaining spinach to prevent it from going to waste. Freeze leftovers that you won't be able to consume within a few days to extend their shelf life and reduce waste.

Use leftover ingredients creatively in future meals. Vegetable scraps can be used to make homemade stocks or soups, while stale bread can be transformed into bread crumbs or croutons. Embrace the challenge of minimizing waste by finding innovative ways to use every part of the ingredients you purchase.

Cooking for a smaller household can be economical with careful planning and budget-conscious strategies. Look for sales and discounts on items you regularly use, such as canned goods, grains, and frozen vegetables. Consider purchasing store brands or generic versions of products to save money without sacrificing quality.

Take advantage of seasonal produce, which is often more affordable and flavorful when it's in season. Visit local farmers' markets or join a community-supported agriculture (CSA) program to access fresh, locally grown fruits and vegetables at competitive prices. Buying directly from farmers not only supports local agriculture but also ensures you're getting high-quality produce at its peak freshness.

Plan meals that are based on affordable ingredients like beans, lentils, and whole grains, which are nutritious and filling. These ingredients can be used in a variety of dishes, from soups and salads to main courses and side dishes. Explore various cooking techniques and flavor pairings to maintain meal variety and enjoyment.

Cooking for one or two people allows for a more personalized culinary experience. Take the time to enjoy the process of preparing meals, from selecting fresh ingredients to experimenting with new recipes. Use cooking as an opportunity to unwind, express creativity, and nourish yourself or your loved ones with wholesome and delicious food.

Embrace the flexibility of cooking for a smaller household by customizing meals to suit your taste preferences and dietary needs. Whether you're cooking for yourself or sharing meals with a partner, savor the opportunity to create memorable dining experiences that cater to your individual preferences.

Cooking for one or two people can be a rewarding experience with the right strategies and approach. By planning meals, minimizing waste, using budget-friendly ingredients, and enjoying the process of cooking, you can create delicious and satisfying meals tailored to your smaller household. Use the opportunity to experiment with new flavors, techniques, and recipes to make the most of your culinary adventures at home.

# Chapter 42. Emergency Preparedness

Emergency preparedness is crucial for every household, ensuring readiness for unexpected situations like natural disasters, power outages, or other disruptions. To stock up on essential supplies without overspending, it's essential to begin with a thorough assessment of your family's needs based on potential risks and your geographic location. Consider local climate-related hazards such as hurricanes or wildfires, as well as infrastructure vulnerabilities like power outages. Tailor your preparations to accommodate the number of people in your household, including special considerations for medications, pets, or elderly family members.

Creating a detailed emergency plan is the next step. This plan should outline how your family will respond to various scenarios, including escape routes, emergency contacts, and a communication strategy to stay connected during a crisis. It's crucial to plan for specific needs, such as medications and medical supplies, that may be necessary during an emergency.

When stocking up on supplies, prioritize essential items that will sustain your family for at least three days. Water is paramount—store at least one gallon per person per day. Consider water purification tablets or filters for additional safety. Non-perishable food items are also essential. Stock up on canned goods, dry goods like rice and pasta, and shelf-stable items that require no refrigeration. Opt for nutritious options such as canned beans, vegetables, fruits, and protein sources like tuna or chicken. Don't forget a manual can opener.

Include a comprehensive first-aid kit with basic supplies such as bandages, gauze, antiseptic wipes, pain relievers, and any necessary medications. Customize the kit to address specific medical needs within your household. Flashlights with extra batteries are crucial for illumination during power outages. Choose energy-efficient LED flashlights that provide long-lasting light. Personal hygiene items like toiletries, hand sanitizer, soap, and disinfectant wipes are important for maintaining cleanliness and sanitation.

Emergency tools such as a multi-tool or Swiss army knife, duct tape, matches or lighters, and a whistle for signaling for help should also be included. Blankets or sleeping bags are necessary for warmth in case of power outages or evacuations. Keep a small amount of emergency cash in small denominations, as ATMs and credit card machines may not be operational during emergencies. Store copies of essential documents—identification, insurance policies, medical records—in a waterproof and fireproof container or secure digital copies on a flash drive.

To manage costs effectively, plan and prioritize your purchases based on your emergency plan. Create a shopping list and acquire essential items gradually to spread out expenses. Take advantage of sales and discounts to purchase non-perishable items in bulk. Consider joining warehouse clubs for cost-effective bulk purchases. Regularly check expiration dates and rotate perishable emergency supplies into your everyday pantry to ensure they are used before they expire. This practice helps maintain a fresh and effective emergency supply stockpile.

It's also beneficial to explore DIY preparedness options, such as assembling your own first aid kits or emergency food packs using items you already have at home. Regularly review and update your emergency supplies and plan at least twice a year. Replace expired items and adjust your plan based on any changes in your household or local risks. Conduct drills or practice your emergency plan with family members to ensure everyone knows what to do during a crisis. Stay informed about local emergency procedures and community resources to enhance your preparedness efforts.

Effective emergency preparedness involves thoughtful planning, strategic purchasing, and ongoing maintenance of your emergency supplies and plan. By prioritizing essential items, shopping wisely, and staying proactive in your preparations, you can ensure your family is ready to handle unexpected situations without overspending. Emergency preparedness
is a continuous process that requires regular review and adaptation to meet the evolving needs of your household and community.

# Chapter 43. Snack and Lunchbox Ideas

Preparing snacks and lunches that are both economical and nutritious is essential for those heading to school, work, or a day out. When it comes to snacks, fresh fruits like apples or berries and cut vegetables such as carrots and cucumber sticks are convenient choices packed with essential vitamins and fiber. Pairing these with hummus or yogurt dip not only enhances flavor but also provides added protein for sustained energy. Trail mix, made from nuts, seeds, and dried fruits, offers versatility and can be customized to personal taste preferences. Buying ingredients in bulk for trail mix is a cost-effective option, ensuring you have a supply on hand for quick and healthy snacking.

Greek yogurt parfaits layered with granola and fresh fruit offer a protein-rich snack that can be prepared ahead of time. This option is perfect for busy mornings when time is limited but nutrition is crucial. Another satisfying snack idea is cheese and whole grain crackers, which provide a balanced combination of protein and carbohydrates. These snacks are easy to pack and ideal for mid-morning or afternoon breaks, keeping hunger at bay without compromising on nutrition.

For budget-friendly lunches, consider using whole-grain wraps or tortillas to create delicious and portable wrap sandwiches. Fill these wraps with lean proteins like grilled chicken or tofu, along with fresh vegetables and spreads such as hummus or avocado for added flavor and nutrients. Mason jar salads provide a trendy and practical lunch option, allowing you to layer dressing, sturdy vegetables, grains, proteins, and leafy greens for a satisfying meal. This method keeps ingredients fresh and ensures your lunch stays delicious until it's time to eat.

Cold pasta salads made with whole grain pasta, mixed veggies, and a light vinaigrette are another hearty lunch option that can be enjoyed cold or at room temperature. These salads are easy to prepare in advance and offer a balanced meal with carbohydrates, vegetables, and optional proteins like grilled chicken or chickpeas. Leftover stir-fries from dinner provide a convenient way to repurpose meals for lunch, combining cooked rice or noodles with leftover vegetables and proteins such as tofu or shrimp. This option is flavorful and ensures nothing goes to waste from your evening meals.

Packing lunches efficiently starts with investing in reusable containers and snack bags that reduce waste and save money over time. Seek containers that are suitable for both microwave reheating and dishwasher cleaning, ensuring convenience. Use smaller containers or dividers within larger ones to portion out snacks and lunches, preventing overeating and minimizing food waste. Preparing snacks and lunches ahead of time, whether on weekends or evenings, ensures you have nutritious options ready to go throughout the week. Wash and chop fruits and vegetables, portion out snacks into individual servings, and assemble meals so they're easy to grab and enjoy. By incorporating these tips and ideas into your routine, you can streamline your snack and lunch preparations, making smart choices that support both your budget and your health.

# Chapter 44. Smart Unit Price Shopping Guide

Understanding and comparing unit prices is a cornerstone of effective grocery shopping, helping consumers make informed decisions that maximize savings without sacrificing quality. Unit price refers to the cost per standard unit of a product, such as per ounce, pound, liter, or other standardized measure. This metric allows shoppers to directly compare the value of products, irrespective of their packaging size or brand, ensuring they get the best deal for their money.

One of the key advantages of comparing unit prices is its ability to provide a consistent basis for evaluating similar products. This consistency is crucial because it eliminates the confusion that can arise from different packaging sizes or promotional offers. For example, a larger package might seem like a better deal at first glance, but calculating the unit price reveals whether it truly offers better value compared to smaller or differently packaged options. This method empowers consumers to make choices that align with their budget and preferences without falling prey to marketing tactics that emphasize bulk purchases without considering actual savings per unit.

To effectively compare unit prices, shoppers can utilize several straightforward strategies. Most grocery stores display unit prices on shelf labels alongside the total price of the item. This makes it convenient to evaluate different brands or sizes of the same product directly in-store. For items where unit prices are not displayed or when comparing products that are not adjacent on the shelf, calculating the unit price manually is straightforward. Simply divide the total price by the quantity (e.g., ounces or pounds) to determine the cost per unit. This approach ensures accuracy and enables shoppers to make quick comparisons even when faced with different packaging options.

When considering bulk purchases, which are often associated with lower unit prices, it's essential to verify the actual savings per unit. While larger quantities typically offer a lower cost per unit, this isn't always the case. Factors such as shelf life, storage space, and personal consumption rates should also be considered. For perishable items or products with expiration dates, purchasing in bulk may not always be practical if it leads to waste due to spoilage. In such cases, opting for smaller quantities that align with immediate needs and consumption patterns may be more cost-effective in the long run.

Moreover, comparing unit prices extends beyond basic groceries to include household essentials, personal care items, and even larger purchases like electronics or appliances. This practice encourages a mindful approach to shopping, where consumers prioritize value and efficiency over impulse buys or misleading promotions. By consistently evaluating unit prices across various product categories, shoppers can develop savvy shopping habits that save both time and money.

Another aspect to consider when comparing unit prices is the balance between quality and quantity. While unit prices provide a clear economic comparison, they do not always reflect factors like product freshness, nutritional content, or overall quality. In some cases, paying a slightly higher unit price for a premium brand or fresher produce may be justified by the enhanced taste, nutritional benefits, or longer shelf life. This decision often comes down to personal preferences and priorities, with some consumers prioritizing value and savings while others prioritize quality and satisfaction.

Furthermore, understanding unit prices can help consumers navigate the complexities of promotions and discounts offered by retailers. For instance, "buy one, get one free" or "50% off" deals may seem attractive initially, but calculating the unit price reveals whether these promotions genuinely offer better value compared to regular-priced items or competing brands. It's essential to remain discerning and not be swayed solely by promotional messaging without verifying the actual savings per unit.

Mastering the art of comparing unit prices empowers consumers to make informed choices that optimize their grocery spending. By leveraging this knowledge, shoppers can confidently navigate supermarket aisles, identify cost-effective options, and prioritize products that align with their budget and preferences. Whether shopping for everyday essentials or making larger purchases, understanding unit prices ensures that every dollar spent delivers maximum value and satisfaction. This approach not only supports financial wellness but also fosters a mindful and strategic approach to shopping that benefits both individuals and families alike.

# Chapter 45. Maximizing Savings with Seasonal Shopping

Maximizing savings through seasonal shopping for fresh produce like vegetables and fruits is a smart strategy that aligns with both budget-conscious shopping and culinary enjoyment. When fruits and vegetables are in peak season, they are not only more abundant but also typically priced lower due to higher supply and reduced transportation costs. You can easily leverage seasonal shopping to maximize savings and enhance your meals throughout the year.

Buying fresh produce at the height of its season allows you to take advantage of lower prices without compromising on quality. Farmers and retailers often offer discounts on seasonal produce because there is a surplus available, making it an ideal time to stock up on your favorite fruits and vegetables. This not only saves you money but also ensures that you are getting the freshest and most flavorful options available.

To extend the benefits of seasonal shopping, consider freezing certain items that are suitable for preservation. Many fruits and vegetables can be frozen for later use, allowing you to enjoy them during the months when they are out of season and more expensive. Freezing berries, for example, preserves their nutritional value and flavor, making them perfect for smoothies, baking, or topping yogurt throughout the year. Similarly, vegetables like peas, corn, and green beans can be blanched and frozen for use in soups, stews, and casseroles during the colder months.

Avoiding products that are out of season is another key aspect of maximizing savings and culinary enjoyment. Out-of-season produce tends to be more expensive because it must be sourced from regions with different growing conditions or imported from other countries, increasing transportation and handling costs. Additionally, fruits and vegetables that are not in season may not taste as fresh or flavorful since they are often picked before they are fully ripe to withstand long-distance travel.

Furthermore, out-of-season produce is more susceptible to spoilage due to its extended travel time and storage conditions. This can result in a shorter shelf life and increased food waste, undermining your efforts to save money and enjoy fresh ingredients. By focusing on seasonal shopping, you can reduce waste and ensure that your meals are made with the best-tasting and most cost-effective ingredients available.

Incorporating seasonal produce into your meal planning can also inspire creativity in the kitchen and introduce variety to your diet. Seasonal fruits and vegetables offer diverse flavors and textures that can enhance both savory and sweet dishes. For example, summer tomatoes are perfect for fresh salads or homemade pasta sauce, while winter squash can be roasted and pureed into comforting soups or added to casseroles for hearty meals.

Seasonal shopping also supports local farmers and promotes sustainability by reducing the environmental impact of long-distance transportation and storage. By purchasing fruits and vegetables that are grown locally and in season, you are supporting agricultural practices that prioritize freshness, flavor, and community health.

Maximizing savings on seasonal shopping for fresh produce involves strategic planning and a commitment to quality and value. By buying fruits and vegetables at the peak of their season, freezing items for future use, and avoiding out-of-season products, you can enjoy delicious meals while saving money and reducing food waste. Seasonal shopping not only benefits your budget and taste buds but also contributes to a sustainable food system that values freshness, flavor, and community well-being.

# Chapter 46. Spend Within Your Budget

Spending within your budget and consistently adding to your savings through smart grocery shopping is not only financially rewarding but also contributes to a sense of accomplishment and confidence in managing your resources effectively. Each month presents an opportunity to strategize and make informed decisions that align with your financial goals, ensuring that your grocery expenses remain within the limits you've set while maximizing the value of every dollar spent.

Setting a budget for your monthly grocery shopping serves as a practical financial tool, helping you allocate resources based on your income, household size, and dietary needs. Begin by assessing your overall financial situation and determining a reasonable amount to allocate towards groceries each month. This budget should account for essential food items as well as any household supplies or personal care products you typically purchase during your grocery trips.

Once your budget is established, the next step is to plan your grocery shopping strategically. Meal planning plays a crucial role in this process, allowing you to create a weekly or biweekly menu based on the ingredients you already have and those you need to purchase. Start by taking inventory of your pantry, refrigerator, and freezer to avoid buying duplicates or unnecessary items. This practice not only prevents food waste but also helps streamline your shopping list to include only what is essential.

When creating your shopping list, prioritize staple items such as grains, beans, pasta, and canned goods that form the foundation of many meals. These items are typically affordable when purchased in bulk or during sales, making them cost-effective choices that contribute to staying within your budget. Additionally, consider seasonal produce, which tends to be fresher, more flavorful, and often less expensive than out-of-season varieties. By aligning your meal planning with seasonal availability, you can capitalize on lower prices and enjoy a wider variety of fruits and vegetables throughout the year.

To further stretch your grocery budget, look for opportunities to save on everyday essentials through coupons, loyalty programs, and store promotions. Many grocery stores offer digital coupons that can be loaded onto your loyalty card or smartphone app, providing instant savings on select items at checkout. Additionally, take advantage of sales events and markdowns on perishable items nearing their expiration dates, as these can often be frozen or used immediately to save money without sacrificing quality.

A key aspect of successful budgeting and savings through grocery shopping is adopting a mindset of mindful consumption. This involves making conscious choices about where and how you spend your money, focusing on value rather than impulse purchases or brand loyalty. Compare prices across different brands and consider store brands or generic alternatives that can be equally nutritious and of comparable quality at a lower cost.

Another strategy to stay within your grocery budget is to limit dining out or ordering takeout, as these expenses can quickly add up and strain your monthly finances. By preparing meals at home with ingredients purchased within your budget, you not only save money but also have more control over portion sizes, ingredients, and overall nutritional content. Batch cooking and meal prepping are effective techniques for saving time and money, allowing you to cook larger quantities of food and portion them out for multiple meals throughout the week.

As you consistently adhere to your budget and prioritize savings through smart grocery shopping, you'll likely experience a sense of achievement and confidence in your financial management skills. Knowing that you are effectively managing your grocery expenses and adding to your savings each month can provide peace of mind and financial security. This positive reinforcement can extend beyond grocery shopping, influencing other aspects of your financial life and enhancing your overall well-being.

Spending within your budget and actively adding to your savings through clever grocery shopping is a practical and empowering approach to financial management. By setting clear financial goals, planning your grocery trips strategically, and making informed purchasing decisions, you can achieve financial stability while enjoying nutritious meals and reducing food waste. Embrace the satisfaction of knowing that each grocery trip contributes to your long-term financial success and enhances your confidence in managing your resources effectively.

# Chapter 47. The Art of Making Food Combinations

Creating delicious and economical meals at home using a combination of grocery store staples and ingredients you already have on hand is both rewarding and practical. By smartly planning your grocery purchases and utilizing versatile items like canned foods and whole ingredients, you can prepare a variety of meals that are not only delicious but also budget-friendly.

It is really interesting to combine grocery store finds with pantry staples to make hearty and nutritious meals at home. When planning your grocery shopping, look for versatile items like canned foods, whole roasted chicken, and basic pantry staples that can be used in multiple dishes throughout the week. This approach not only saves time and money but also ensures that you always have the ingredients on hand to whip up a delicious and healthy meal at a moment's notice.

By experimenting with different flavor combinations and meal ideas, you can expand your culinary repertoire and enjoy homemade meals that rival those found in restaurants. Whether you're preparing a quick lunch, a family dinner, or a weekend brunch, combining grocery store finds with pantry staples allows you to create meals that are both budget-friendly and satisfying for everyone at the table.

**Canned Food Creations**

Canned foods are convenient pantry staples that can serve as the foundation for many quick and satisfying meals. Items like tuna, luncheon meat, beans, and vegetables can be transformed into delicious sandwiches, salads, and more. For example, canned tuna mixed with mayonnaise or Greek yogurt, chopped celery, and a dash of mustard makes a tasty filling for sandwiches or wraps. You can add lettuce, tomato, and cheese to complete a nutritious and easy-to-make meal.

Luncheon meat, such as canned beef or turkey, can be thinly sliced and layered with cheese, lettuce, and tomato between slices of whole-grain bread for a simple yet satisfying sandwich. For a hot option, consider heating slices of luncheon meat in a skillet and serving them with scrambled eggs and toast for a hearty breakfast or brunch.

Canned beans are versatile additions to soups, stews, salads, and wraps. Rinse and drain canned chickpeas or black beans, then toss them with olive oil, lemon juice, garlic, and your choice of herbs for a quick and nutritious bean salad. You can also use them as a filling for burritos or tacos, combined with salsa, cheese, lettuce, and sour cream for a flavorful and budget-friendly dinner option.

**Utilizing Whole Roasted Chicken**
A whole roasted chicken from the grocery store is a versatile ingredient that can be used to create multiple meals throughout the week. Start by enjoying roasted chicken breast with steamed vegetables and mashed potatoes for a classic and comforting meal. Leftover chicken can be shredded and used in a variety of dishes, such as chicken salad sandwiches, wraps, or added to soups and casseroles for added protein and flavor.

To make a quick and satisfying chicken stir-fry, sauté leftover chicken with mixed vegetables (like bell peppers, broccoli, and carrots) in a skillet with soy sauce and garlic. Serve over cooked rice or noodles for a complete and nutritious meal that can be made in under 30 minutes.

For a lighter option, use shredded chicken breast in a refreshing salad with mixed greens, cherry tomatoes, cucumber, avocado, and a drizzle of balsamic vinaigrette. You can also toss shredded chicken with pasta, pesto, and cherry tomatoes for a flavorful pasta dish that is perfect for a quick weeknight dinner.

**Burger and Sandwich Creations**

Making burgers and sandwiches at home allows you to customize flavors and ingredients while saving money compared to dining out. Start with ground beef or turkey purchased from the grocery store and season with your favorite herbs and spices to create flavorful burger patties. Grill or cook the patties in a skillet until cooked through, then assemble with lettuce, tomato, onion, and cheese on whole grain buns for a satisfying and wholesome meal.

For a vegetarian option, use canned black beans or chickpeas as the base for homemade veggie burgers. Mash the beans with breadcrumbs, eggs, chopped vegetables (like bell peppers and onions), and spices (such as cumin and chili powder) before forming into patties and cooking until golden brown. Serve on whole wheat buns with avocado, lettuce, and salsa for a nutritious and delicious meatless meal.

Sandwiches can also be made using leftover roasted chicken or canned tuna mixed with mayonnaise, celery, and spices. Add lettuce, tomato, and cheese between slices of whole grain bread for a simple and satisfying lunch option that can be made ahead and packed for on-the-go meals.

## Some Easy Dessert Ideas

**Fruit and Yogurt Parfait:** Layer Greek yogurt with canned fruit (like pineapple or peaches) and granola in glasses or bowls. Repeat layers and top with granola for added crunch.

**Homemade Berry Compote:** Simmer frozen berries with sugar and lemon juice until thickened. Serve warm over pancakes, yogurt, or ice cream.

**No-Bake Cheesecake:** Mix cream cheese, sugar, and vanilla extract. Press graham cracker crumbs mixed with melted butter into a pie dish or individual cups for the crust. Spread the cream cheese mixture over the crust and refrigerate until set. Top with canned fruit, like cherry pie filling, before serving.

**Chocolate and Peanut Butter Bars:** Melt peanut butter, chocolate chips, and butter together. Stir in powdered sugar and graham cracker crumbs until well combined. Press into a baking dish and refrigerate until firm. Cut into bars and serve chilled.

**Fruit Crumble:** Toss drained canned fruit or thawed frozen fruit with sugar and placed in a baking dish. Mix oats, flour, brown sugar, and butter until crumbly, then sprinkle over the fruit. Bake until golden brown and bubbly. Serve warm with vanilla ice cream.

# Chapter 48. Some Important Considerations

In the hustle and bustle of daily life, grocery shopping often becomes a routine task, yet it holds untapped potential for significant savings and efficiency gains. Beyond merely picking items off shelves, strategic grocery shopping involves thoughtful considerations that extend beyond the store's aisles. Learning the art of clever grocery shopping means uncovering hidden aspects that can impact your finances, time management, and overall well-being.

Clever grocery shopping is a multifaceted endeavor that extends beyond simply filling a shopping cart. By incorporating considerations such as fuel costs, time efficiency, energy conservation, and smart cost evaluation into your shopping routine, you can maximize savings while enhancing your overall well-being. Embrace strategic planning, prioritize efficiency, and make informed purchasing decisions to transform grocery shopping into a financially savvy and rewarding experience. By doing so, you'll not only optimize your household budget but also contribute to a more sustainable and balanced lifestyle.

**Consideration of Fuel Costs**
One of the often-overlooked aspects of grocery shopping is the impact of fuel costs. Many of us drive to our preferred grocery store without considering the distance or the fuel consumed in the process. It's natural to seek out cheaper groceries, but driving long distances to save a few dollars can sometimes nullify those savings when fuel expenses are factored in. Therefore, it's prudent to evaluate the overall cost-effectiveness of where you shop. Opting for a closer grocery store or combining errands to minimize driving distances can result in significant savings over time.

## Embrace Time-Saving Options

Time is a precious commodity, and efficient grocery shopping can help reclaim valuable hours. When selecting groceries, prioritize items that require minimal preparation time. Quick-cooking grains, pre-cut vegetables, and ready-to-eat proteins like canned beans or rotisserie chicken not only streamline meal preparation but also reduce the energy (both electricity and gas) expended in the kitchen. This approach not only saves money on utility bills but also frees up time for other activities or relaxation.

## Harness Natural Light

An often-overlooked aspect of household economics is energy usage during meal preparation. By planning and preparing meals during daylight hours, you can harness natural light, thereby reducing your reliance on electric lighting. This simple adjustment not only cuts down on electricity costs but also aligns with sustainable living practices. Additionally, utilizing natural light can create a more pleasant cooking environment, enhancing the overall culinary experience.

## Efficient and Stress-Free Shopping

Efficiency in grocery shopping goes beyond the selection of products. Planning ahead and creating a detailed shopping list based on weekly meal plans can prevent impulse purchases and unnecessary trips to the store. This approach not only saves time but also reduces stress and fatigue associated with last-minute shopping. Consider utilizing grocery delivery or curbside pickup services, which have become increasingly available, to further streamline the shopping process. These services not only save time but also minimize the temptation to make impulse buys, ultimately contributing to better financial management.

## Avoid False Economies

While saving money is a priority for many shoppers, it's essential to avoid false economies that may lead to higher costs or health implications in the long run. Opting for cheaper, processed foods over fresh and nutritious alternatives may seem economical initially but can contribute to higher healthcare costs and reduced well-being over time. Strike a balance by prioritizing quality and nutritional value when making purchasing decisions. Investing in wholesome ingredients and balanced meals not only supports overall health but also promotes long-term financial savings by reducing the risk of future health complications.

**Comprehensive Cost Evaluation**

When assessing the cost-effectiveness of grocery shopping, it's crucial to consider the holistic impact of your choices. Beyond the price of groceries, factor in transportation costs, time spent, and potential savings on utilities. A slightly higher price at a nearby store may prove more economical when these factors are taken into account. Moreover, consider the environmental impact of your shopping habits. Opting for locally sourced produce and goods not only supports the local economy but also reduces carbon emissions associated with long-distance transportation.

# Chapter 49: Understanding Store Layouts and Strategies

Navigating grocery stores efficiently involves understanding their layouts and the strategies employed to influence consumer behavior. Store layouts are meticulously designed to encourage specific shopping patterns, such as placing essential items at the back to increase exposure to other products. By familiarizing yourself with common store layouts—like grid, loop, and racetrack designs—you can streamline your shopping trips.

Stores strategically place high-demand items, like milk and eggs, at the back to encourage customers to walk through aisles filled with other products, increasing the likelihood of impulse purchases. End-cap displays often showcase promotional items or seasonal products to catch shoppers' attention. These displays are prime real estate for highlighting new products or offering special discounts, enticing customers to make unplanned purchases.

Understanding the layout of your preferred grocery store helps optimize your shopping experience. Start by planning your route through the store, beginning with fresh produce, dairy, and meats typically located along the store's perimeter. This strategy minimizes the need to backtrack and reduces exposure to tempting, but unnecessary, items in central aisles. Digital store maps or smartphone apps are valuable tools for locating specific products efficiently, saving time, and preventing frustration.

Store layouts are designed with consumer psychology in mind, utilizing colors, lighting, and music to create a pleasant shopping environment while subtly influencing purchasing decisions. Warm lighting and soft music may encourage shoppers to linger, potentially leading to additional purchases. Meanwhile, strategic placement of everyday essentials encourages frequent visits and increases customer loyalty.

To optimize your shopping experience, consider creating a detailed shopping list based on planned meals and household needs. This proactive approach reduces impulse buys and ensures you only purchase items that align with your budget and dietary preferences. If possible, shop during off-peak hours to avoid crowds and long checkout lines, further enhancing efficiency.

By understanding store layouts and the strategies employed to influence consumer behavior, shoppers can make informed decisions and navigate grocery stores more efficiently. Recognizing the impact of placement, promotions, and consumer psychology empowers individuals to stay focused on their shopping goals, save time, and effectively manage their grocery budgets. Ultimately, mastering store layouts transforms grocery shopping from a routine task into a strategic endeavor, enabling consumers to shop smarter and more economically.

# Chapter 50: Eco-Friendly Grocery Shopping Practices

In today's world, where sustainability is increasingly important, adopting eco-friendly grocery shopping practices not only reduces environmental impact but also aligns with ethical consumerism. Choose products that have minimal or recyclable packaging whenever possible. Many grocery stores now offer bulk sections where you can bring your own containers for items like grains, nuts, and spices, reducing single-use plastics. Look for products packaged in materials that are easily recyclable or compostable, and consider purchasing items in larger quantities to minimize packaging waste.

Choose locally sourced and organic products whenever possible. Locally grown produce and goods typically have a smaller carbon footprint since they travel shorter distances to reach the store shelves. Organic farming practices reduce the use of synthetic pesticides and fertilizers, promoting healthier soil and water quality. By supporting local farmers and producers, you contribute to the local economy and sustainable agriculture.

Combat food waste by planning meals and purchasing only what you need. Make use of leftovers and imperfect produce, which are often sold at a discount or can be creatively incorporated into meals. Consider composting food scraps to reduce landfill waste and enrich the soil for gardening or community projects.

Incorporate more plant-based foods into your diet. Plant-based diets typically exert a lower environmental footprint compared to diets that are high in animal products. Reduce meat consumption and explore plant-based protein sources like legumes, tofu, and nuts, which require fewer resources to produce and often have a smaller carbon footprint.

Purchase fruits and vegetables that are in season locally. Seasonal produce is fresher, tastier, and often more affordable. It also supports agricultural diversity and reduces the energy-intensive process of transporting out-of-season produce from distant locations. Embrace the variety and flavors of each season while reducing environmental impact.

Bring reusable bags and containers for grocery shopping. Keep a stash of reusable bags in your car or near your front door to ensure they're always handy. Opt for durable, washable produce bags for fruits and vegetables instead of using single-use plastic bags provided by the store.

Stay informed about environmental issues related to food production and distribution. Educate yourself about certifications and labels that indicate sustainable practices, such as USDA Organic, Fair Trade, or Marine Stewardship Council (MSC) for seafood. Share your knowledge and enthusiasm with friends and family to encourage broader adoption of eco-friendly shopping habits.

By incorporating eco-friendly practices into your grocery shopping routine, you contribute to environmental conservation and support sustainable agriculture. Each small step—whether it's choosing reusable bags, reducing food waste, or supporting local farmers—makes a positive impact. Embracing eco-friendly grocery shopping practices not only benefits the planet but also promotes a healthier lifestyle and encourages ethical consumerism. Together, we can make a difference in preserving our natural resources for future generations.

# Chapter 51: Grocery Shopping for Special Diets

Grocery shopping for special diets requires careful planning and understanding of dietary restrictions and preferences. Whether you follow a vegan, nut-free, sugar-free, salt-free, gluten-free, dairy-free, or other specialized diet, Begin by educating yourself about the principles and requirements of the specific diet you follow or are considering adopting. For example, a vegan diet excludes all animal products, while a gluten-free diet avoids gluten-containing grains like wheat, barley, and rye. Each diet has its own unique challenges and opportunities, influencing food choices and meal planning.

Plan your meals based on nutrient-rich whole foods that align with your dietary needs. Include a variety of fruits, vegetables, whole grains, legumes, nuts, seeds, and plant-based proteins in a balanced diet. Check ingredient labels carefully to avoid hidden animal-derived ingredients or gluten-containing additives.

Familiarize yourself with sections of the grocery store that cater to special diets, such as the gluten-free aisle or plant-based alternatives. Explore local markets, health food stores, and online retailers that offer a wide selection of specialty products and ingredients tailored to your dietary preferences.

Opt for whole, unprocessed foods whenever possible. Fresh fruits and vegetables, whole grains like quinoa and brown rice, and legumes such as lentils and chickpeas form the foundation of many specialized diets. These foods are naturally free from animal products and gluten, offering nutritional benefits and culinary versatility.

Learn to decipher food labels to identify potential allergens or ingredients that may not align with your dietary restrictions. Look for certified vegan, gluten-free, or allergen-free labels that provide assurance of product safety and compliance with dietary guidelines.

Experiment with alternative ingredients and substitutes to recreate favorite recipes without compromising taste or nutritional value. Replace animal-based proteins with plant-based alternatives like tofu, tempeh, or seitan in vegan dishes. Explore gluten-free flours and baking mixes to make bread, desserts, and other baked goods suitable for a gluten-free diet.

Utilize meal planning and batch cooking techniques to streamline grocery shopping and meal preparation. Prepare large batches of meals that comply with your dietary needs, portioning them for easy reheating throughout the week. Batch cooking ensures you always have convenient, nutritious options on hand and reduces the temptation to stray from your dietary goals.

Connect with online forums, social media groups, or local community organizations that cater to individuals following similar dietary patterns. Share recipe ideas, shopping tips, and support with others facing similar challenges and successes on their journey to maintain a special diet.

Consult registered dietitians, nutritionists, or healthcare providers specializing in dietary counseling for personalized guidance. They can offer tailored recommendations to ensure your special diet meets nutritional requirements and supports overall health and well-being.

Grocery shopping for special diets requires dedication, knowledge, and creativity to navigate effectively. By embracing whole foods, reading labels diligently, and utilizing alternative ingredients, you can enjoy a diverse and satisfying diet that aligns with your dietary preferences and health goals. With careful planning and community support, managing a special diet becomes a rewarding journey toward optimal health and well-being.

# Chapter 52: Last But Not Least

Grocery shopping is not just a chore; it's a fundamental part of our daily lives and essential for nourishing ourselves and our families with quality, healthy foods. In today's world, where living costs can be a concern, being mindful of our grocery expenses is crucial. However, with the right strategies, grocery shopping can be more than just a task—it can be a satisfying and even enjoyable experience that positively impacts our overall well-being.

When we approach grocery shopping with planning and careful consideration, we empower ourselves to make smart choices that align with our budget and dietary needs. By creating and sticking to a shopping list, we ensure that we purchase only what we need, reducing the risk of impulse buys and unnecessary spending. This thoughtful approach not only saves money but also contributes to a sense of accomplishment and control over our finances.

Saving money on groceries allows us to live comfortably within our means. It frees up resources for other important aspects of life, whether it's investing in experiences, saving for the future, or simply reducing financial stress. Knowing that we are making informed decisions about our grocery purchases can bring a sense of satisfaction and peace of mind.

Moreover, buying smartly means more than just looking at prices. It involves understanding product quality, choosing nutritious options, and sometimes exploring alternatives like generic brands or bulk purchases that offer better value. These choices not only save money but also contribute to our overall health and well-being.

Furthermore, grocery shopping can be an opportunity to explore new foods, flavors, and cooking techniques. Whether it's trying seasonal produce, experimenting with ethnic ingredients, or making homemade staples, embracing variety adds excitement to our culinary experiences. Engaging in this exploration with family and friends can turn grocery shopping into a social and enjoyable activity.

In essence, grocery shopping is more than just acquiring food—it's about nurturing ourselves and our loved ones, managing our resources wisely, and finding joy in the everyday essentials. By approaching it with mindfulness, planning, and a sense of adventure, we can transform this routine task into a positive and rewarding part of our lives. Let's embrace the journey of smart grocery shopping, where every choice we make contributes not only to our physical well-being but also to our happiness and satisfaction.

So keep enjoying your grocery shopping, keep saving money, and keep buying smartly. You're not just stocking your pantry—you're enriching your life with quality, nourishing foods and fostering a sense of fulfillment in every meal. Enjoy the process, savor the flavors, and relish in the knowledge that your thoughtful approach to grocery shopping is making a positive difference in your life.

www.ingramcontent.com/pod-product-compliance
Lightning Source LLC
Chambersburg PA
CBHW071024250726

48653CB00005B/1701

*9798329696806*